Show Us the Money

SHOW US THE MONEY

The
___
Politics and
___
Process of
___
Alternative
___
Budgets

CHO!CES: A Coalition for Social Justice
Canadian Centre for Policy Alternatives

ARBEITER RING
Winnipeg

Arbeiter Ring Publishing
2-91 Albert Street
Winnipeg, Manitoba
Canada R3B 1G5

Copyright © 1998

Printed in Canada

Canadian Cataloguing in Publication Data

Main entry under title:

Show us the money: the politics and process of alternative
   budgets

ISBN 1-894037-03-0

1. Budget—Canada—Citizen participation.
I.Choices (Association). II. Canadian Centre for
Policy Alternatives.

HJ2055.S46 1998   352.4'8'0971   C98-920145-7

Contents

Acknowledgements

Show Us the Money is the fruit of nearly a year's labours, and owes everything to the contributions of some very generous people. First, thanks to all of the activists involved in the Alternative Federal Budget project, the Canadian Centre for Policy Alternatives, and the members of the Ottawa Steering Committee. Special thanks to Cho!ces and to the members of the Winnipeg Working Group, who lent their support early on to an ambitious idea. Great appreciation goes to Doug Smith and Mike Maunder, who constructed the basis of the workshop—and wrote the bulk of the book—out of some pretty nebulous concepts. Thanks to Esyllt Jones, Phil Lancaster and Angeline Simbandumwe, the members of the coordinating committee who hung in to finish what was originally begun. To John Loxley, for his characteristically succinct introduction, and for all the guidance he's given to alternative budgets along the way. Jim Stanford explained how to put budgets together in a fiscal planning spreadsheet. Denise Doherty-Delorme and her colleagues at the Canadian Federation of Students developed the elegant timeline which appears in chapter 3 (and to which Phil added some colour), and also gave many useful comments in their capacity as guinea pigs. Way back when, Shauna McKinnon compiled a glossary of budget terms, the first version of the excellent glossary completed by Fletcher Barager and Doug Smith. Fletcher must also be thanked for being the first to lead a workshop with this material. Doug is thanked for integrating the advice that came out of that workshop. Victor Dobchuk contributed ideas on working with the media. And George Harris, veteran of several alternative civic budgets in Winnipeg, provided valuable information on that subject.

Along with some of the people mentioned above, Elizabeth Carlyle, Robert Chernomas, Shirley Lord, and Greg Selinger also tested this material as they led workshops across the country in 1997 and 1998, and gave valuable feedback.

John Samson and Todd Scarth at Arbeiter Ring did the editing and design, and then they did it again, after a catastrophic computer meltdown. Thanks to Simon "What would Alexander Rodchenko do here?" Hughes for co-designing the cover. And to Illustrating Queen Anna Scott, who was able to make even federal budgets look pretty cool and funky—no mean feat.

The Canadian Labour Congress, the Canadian Association of University Teachers, the Canadian Conference of Catholic Bishops and the Confédération des syndicats nationaux gave generous financial support to the Alternative Federal Budget project, without which this book would not have been written.

As is said at Cho!ces, "kudos" above all to the many people across the country interested in alternative budgets, and who have come out to workshops to learn more about the politics and mechanics of alternative budgets. *Show Us the Money* was written with one simple conviction in mind—ordinary people have the knowledge and capability to create and sustain a more just economy. Take it, take it apart, use it however you can.

Introduction

The preparation of government budgets is generally considered to be a job for technical experts, not for ordinary Canadians. Governments of all ideological stripes have found it politically convenient to perpetuate this myth: the less people know the less they can challenge the prevailing political orthodoxy as expressed in the budget. And in recent years the budgets of all levels of government have become a major arena of political struggle. Important public sector services and the skilled public sector jobs needed to deliver them have been slashed in the name of "responsible budgeting." People have been told that there really are no alternatives, the cuts were and continue to be absolutely necessary, a matter of technical necessity unrelated to the political agenda that drives them.

In the early 1990s, Cho!ces, a Winnipeg based coalition for social justice, began to challenge this view, arguing that there were in fact many alternatives to the cut and slash mentality of reactionary governments. Keeping people away from the budgetary process, Cho!ces argued, was necessary in order to keep people in ignorance for, as Rudolph Goldscheid argued over 75 years ago, you have to do violence to the facts in order to do violence to the people. So Cho!ces began to get people involved in preparing alternative budgets at the provincial, civic and school board levels demonstrating, concretely, that there are alternative, humane, and enlightened approaches to public policy which are, at the same time, fiscally responsible. An important feature of these alternative budgets is the participatory manner in which they are put together, drawing on volunteers from all walks of life and especially those most affected by different aspects of the budgets in question. Opening up the process enables people to see how budgets are put together, how trade offs are made and to appreciate the real versus imagined budgetary constraints that governments have to work within. This is an enormously enlightening process for everybody involved, including so-called technical people (it is still useful to have a few of these involved!) who rarely get to work alongside the people affected by their work.

From a very early stage, Cho!ces began to run a series of budget workshops or schools as a means of broadening the understanding of basic budgeting as well as spreading its political message. Indeed, these get-togethers became a major way of creating involvement in the process and of building support for a fiscally sound progressive political agenda across the country. Out of one of these workshops came the idea for an alternative federal budget which, since 1995, has been prepared by activists across the country under the leadership of Cho!ces and the Canadian Centre for Policy Alternatives (CCPA), Ottawa. Budget schools helped, in some small way at least, to encourage activists elsewhere in Canada to prepare alternative provincial budgets.

The main object of this book is to put together some of the notes developed in budget schools and workshops so they can be more easily available to activists. Since the alternative budget process, and especially the schools and workshops, is a very interactive process, what follows can truly be said to be a product of input from Canadians right across the country and not simply of Cho!ces or the CCPA. *Show Us the Money* is not intended to present a blueprint for people to follow or to answer all the questions that are likely to arise when preparing alternative budgets in any given place. Rather, it is structured to give some basic background on budgeting and to expose people to ideas which have been found helpful in the past. It raises many questions, the answers to which should help guide people towards budgets suitable for their specific needs and their unique situations.

The central message of this book is that budgets are, above all, political documents and that people should not be afraid of them. Democratizing the budget process is important if we are to effectively resist the platform of the neo-conservatives and replace it with a public policy more in tune with needs of ordinary Canadians.

—John Loxley

1. How to Use This Book

Well, read it. The main text of this book (excluding the facilitators' notes, found in the sidebars of the page) is for anyone who wants to learn more about the Alternative Federal Budget (AFB) or alternative budgets and the budgeting process in general. It uses the 1998 AFB as an example, but the concepts are applicable to other levels of government budgets. Reading through *Show Us the Money* is like attending a workshop. There are exercises with each section, asking you to apply what you've learned in the previous discussion, and to think creatively about using alternative budgets as political tools.

As a Workshop Leader

This book is also designed to be used as a guide for anyone who wants to lead their own alternative budget workshop. We start you off with some information about adult education, and throughout you will see notes to facilitators in the sidebars of many of the pages. Each facilitator's note will be indicated by this icon:

These notes are meant to guide facilitators through the material, to explain some of the exercises, and to anticipate some of the difficulties you might encounter. This particular alternative budget workshop, in various formats, was tried out in about twenty alternative budget workshops across the country in 1997-1998, and the notes in the sidebars reflect some of the feedback we received from people who attended those workshops.

You'll also find supporting materials such as overheads and handouts appended at the end of the book. They are designed so as to be easily photocopied. We have given tips on when to use overheads, and when to direct participants to their handouts, by using the following icons:

If you encounter words or phrases that are unfamiliar to you, check the glossary for definitions.

SO, YOU WANT TO GET INVOLVED IN AN ALTERNATIVE BUDGET WORKSHOP

 As facilitator, your work will begin before the workshop. Ideally, the facilitator will have a good idea of who the participants are. Try to find out some basic information about the people you'll be working with. Who are the participants? What are their affiliations? Their reasons for attending? Their goals? A few phone calls can get a sense of this.

And don't forget the obvious things: make sure there's coffee, juice, name tags, flip charts, an overhead projector, and so on.

The first hour of the workshop is designed to build safety—basic description and objectives of the workshop, introductions, some really simple budget terms, and a game, "The Price is Right." Allow everyone to begin to get to know one another and to see that, amongst them, they have knowledge already and that the workshop is going to be a participatory process. Setting a respectful tone in this first exercise will get the workshop off on the right foot. Be sure to highlight the objectives of the workshop, including participants' objectives.

Start by introducing yourself and the four objectives

Whatever your background, whether you're an economics professor or a community activist, you have something unique to bring to the workshop—yourself, your own knowledge and practical experience in dealing with the issues of wealth, poverty, power, and struggle that are at the core of the AFB. You don't have to be an expert. It helps to remember that the words "expert," "experience," and "experiment" all come from the same root. Real education focuses on the experience that everyone in a workshop brings, and their openness to experimenting together, and that process begins with you.

A teacher was once defined as someone who reads the text one page ahead of the students. If you read and consider this book before leading a workshop, you'll be okay on the content of the budget. There are also "experts" you can consult at Cho!ces, the Canadian Centre for Policy Alternatives, or maybe an economics department, a union, or someone else nearby. But the pages that follow try to convince you of something deeper—that your job is to bring out your own experience and the experience of the people attending the workshop. You should strive to be a facilitator, not a teacher. Facilitate means "to make facile, to make easy." A facilitator strives to make learning easier for participants, to make participation easier, and then the learning happens—for you, as well as the other participants.

Education done this way is thus very democratic. These pages are designed to give you a grounding in this approach to education, particularly as you design your own alternative budget workshop. They should not be thought of as a text that you follow from A to B to C. Play with the activities. Know who your participants are and what they bring to the workshop in terms of knowledge, experience, expectations, and needs. Look at your own knowledge and experience. And then plan your workshop. It will not be the workshop done by the economist in St. John's or by the activist in Edmonton. It will be yours, and your participants'. And that's the best workshop there could be.

To help you plan, here are ten principles for democratic education. There are dozens more. But if out of these ten, you can find three or four you really endorse, then use them as you make your own plans.

TEN GUIDELINES FOR DEMOCRATIC EDUCATION

1. Be Concerned with Learning, Not Teaching

Learners come with a whole array of expectations, real life concerns, pressures and experiences. You must link to their world, not yours.

The process of learning is controlled by the learner, not the facilitator. Thus, you can be lecturing about Adam Smith, but the learner is thinking about whether they left their car lights on. A person in that mode might momentarily click into what you were saying if you started comparing supply and demand to the amount of electricity in a car battery, but for the most part they won't be getting much out of the experience. As a facilitator you should start where learners are and bring them towards your knowledge, rather than starting where you are, and expecting them to come along. This means an important part of the workshop is the first half-hour, listening to participants' introductions and objectives for the workshop.

2. Learning is a Cooperative and Collaborative Process

As Brazilian educator Paulo Friere demonstrated, education is not a process where eager learners sit, and you pour knowledge into their heads. They are not empty vessels waiting to be filled. Think of knowledge pouring out from the group. Your job is to facilitate the flowing of this knowledge. You should drink heartily from that river as well; you have something to learn from these participants. Trust them, trust their intentions to learn (they have after all given up a chunk of their time to be here). This collaborative principle is ideally modelled by having the group sit in a circle, with frequent break-outs into small groups.

3. The Basic Ground Rule Should be Respect for All

It's good to have simple ground rules, and the most basic is Respect. The major principle of democratic education is to respect the contribution that everyone in a workshop brings. As facilitator, you need to model that respect—respect for others, respect for yourself. Respect learners by having your material ready, by being on time, and respect them by really hearing what they have to say as well. Listen more, talk less. A good tool for this is the "sharing circle" in which you go around a circle and allow each person to speak in turn. There is no debate or discussion, just listening to, and respecting, each person as they speak. Remember, hearing someone and understanding their position doesn't mean you agree with them.

4. Learning Involves More than Just the Mind

The body needs movement, not just sitting. Occasionally throw in a physical activity. Emotions need to be engaged. Good learning and good teaching involve passion. Perhaps there are people in your group who can really relate what job creation means to them personally because they've been out of work for years. When learners feel strongly, it strengthens learning for everyone. With budgets, learners need to handle them, crunch the numbers, discuss them—not sit and listen to an expert. AFB workshops tend to be lecture ori-

of the workshop. Give a brief history of how the AFB has been put together. Describe the way in which the idea of an alternative budget arose as a response to politicians who claimed they had no choice but to introduce neo-conservative policies. The AFB is not meant to be the only alternative, but its existence makes it clear that there are progressive alternatives. Stress the importance of the participatory process by which the AFB has been put together, and that, although objectives 1-3 certainly require a lot of mastery of material, objective 4 asks each of them to be a participant in the process and to perhaps provide new insights, even if they believe that their budget knowledge is not the greatest.

Tell participants why you are there, and then ask everyone to introduce themselves, perhaps mentioning an organization or a community activity they're involved in, and to answer the question, "If there was one thing you wanted in a federal budget (or whatever kind of budget you're creating), what would it be?" Write their answers on the flip chart.

ented so we've incorporated activities into the workshop. And there is always room for you to plan new activities.

5. There Are Many Different Learning Styles

Think about the different ways of assembling an IKEA bookcase. Some people open the box, grab a screwdriver and start putting it together immediately. Call them hands-on learners. Some spread out all the parts, read all the instructions two or three times and then start. They're contemplatives. Once the bookcase is constructed, you have to set it up. Some people, before they start, make a sketch, measure the space and then just put it there. They're planners. But others, once it's there, think it doesn't quite fit and end up rearranging all the furniture to put it somewhere else. They're see-ers, they have to see it. Are you a hands-on doer? A contemplative? A planner? A see-er? Or a bit of each? All are valid techniques for learning, and all need to be in your workshop.

6. Provide Opportunities for Reflection

Reflection is the most important and usually least regarded aspect of learning. People need time to process what they're learning. They need to internalize it into their own world, link it with what they already know. Sometimes, we can be so caught up in our lecture, bombarding people with knowledge; or so caught up in our neat activities, occupying them constantly with new things to do, that we forget to provide time for people to absorb and reflect. This time should be provided at the end of each workshop and is a vital part of the learning, not just something tacked on at the end. It's good to structure reflection activities throughout the workshop. Don't be afraid to sit in a circle and just ask people to reflect on what's happened so far; use their observations to modify the rest of the workshop.

7. "The Best-Laid Plans of Mice and Men ..."

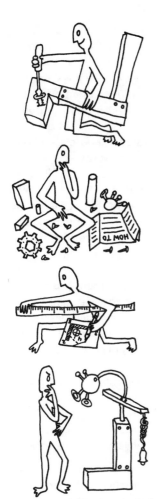

"There are many different learning styles ..."

Plans often go astray, as Robbie Burns said. Don't be afraid to abandon your tightly scheduled agenda and spend a longer time talking about something that interests your group. This is not a sign of personal failure as a facilitator, but a sign that you're responding to the real needs of learners. The agenda of the meeting is there as a supportive structure, but the facilitator's main concern must be with the learners, not the agenda. Perhaps you're an economist and can really explain what globalization means, even though it's not technically part of the workshop. That's great; that's a gift you bring to the workshop. There are other gifts too that the learners bring. Use them, but recognize that you'll likely changing the best-laid plans. That's okay. Be flexible.

8. Make the Workshop a Safe Place

If there is one thing that is the single most important job of a facilitator, it is to make the workshop a safe place for participants. Show that you respect them. Praise their efforts. Discourage judgemental discussions and "right" answers. Model these behaviours. Create an atmosphere where they feel able to share their knowledge and their stories. Facilitation is not indoctrination. In a learning situation, the facilitator has power over the learners. You abuse that power if you use it to convince and persuade learners of your point of view. By doing that, you also make the workshop an unsafe place for people to express contrary views. Encourage contrariness. Trust the group to come up with some new answers, not just the standard answers.

9. Use Lots of Small Group Work

One of the best ways to create safety is by doing lots of small group work. Many people will talk in a group of five who would never talk in the large group. Pairs are even better. You lose central control when people divide into groups, but this is fine. Learning is individual. It's not necessary that everything that happens in a small group come back to a plenary session where everyone listens to what Group A decided, Group B, and on and on. The learning happened in that small group and the learning in each small group was different. It's not necessary, or even possible, that everyone learn the same thing. When using small groups, it's best, if possible, that you not be a part of a group, so you can wander from group to group, hear what they're doing, and gently get them back on track if necessary.

10. What If Things Go Wrong?

Everybody preparing a workshop has anxiety. What if there's someone smarter than me who has all the answers? What if someone wants to dominate the discussion? What if it becomes clear that I'm really just one page ahead of everyone? What if people ask questions I can't answer? What if we don't cover everything?

When you see democratic education as facilitating the group, all of these problems are normal. The person with all the answers? Use them as an expert to answer the questions you can't (or even the ones you can). The person who dominates? The group will be as annoyed as you are, use this as a chance to discuss ground rules like respect for all. Use small groups and go around the circle every now and then to solve the opposite problem—getting input from the person who never speaks. When it becomes clear you're not a genius? Make it clear at the start that you need participation to help. Model being vulnerable—it makes others feel safe to question and experiment. When people ask something you don't know, say, "I don't know."

For the last anxiety—not covering everything—see the next section.

Do what you can to make the workshop free. Hold it in a building where people feel welcome. We've found that it really helps, if possible, to provide lunch on a full day. If you must charge, keep the price as low as possible so that everyone who is interested can attend. Get union locals and community groups and anyone else who might be interested the information early so that they can spread the word. Check out what else is going on in your community before you set the date to avoid scheduling conflicts with other events that possible participants might want to attend.

TIMING: THE MAJOR CONSIDERATION IN PLANNING

There is never enough time in workshops. Almost inevitably, something that's designed to take two hours takes three hours. This is because adult learners are demanding. They want material related to them. They have their own views. These things need to be honoured. For unlike the education of children, adults are generally able to make their desires known. With children, the unfortunate reality is that teachers can often simply move ahead with the program, even though many of the children may be disengaged or do not understand. This is not a good thing to do, but it happens often in the teaching of children. It doesn't happen so often with adults because they have a way of making their desires known, either overtly or covertly. The end result is that, if you are going to be responsive to the needs of your audience, you are inevitably going to move slower than you planned. For these reasons, your first decision should be your workshop agenda.

The workshop given here is designed as a primer in economic theory and current politics as they relate to the AFB. It takes two full days to go through it thoroughly and without rushing. Facilitators' notes at the start of most of the sections give you an indication of how much time to allow for that section. Roughly, chapters 1 through 6 should be covered the first day, and 7 through 9 the second. Please note that the shortest sections in the book in fact require the most time in a workshop, as they are intended to generate lots of discussion. If in fact you have only nine hours (for instance Friday night and Saturday), then it is best to choose which aspects of the material you wish to focus on. For example, will your participants be more interested in the content of the AFB, or in economic literacy? Will they want to spend more time planning for an alternative budget process of their own, or talking about popularization or mobilization? You can leave out sections of the workshop accordingly, or modify the material we've provided. Remember, the result you are aiming for is to get people involved in dealing with budgets. Your workshop is only one building block in that process.

When planning a workshop, it is always best to make your best plans, and then add a third to everything. So if you're planning an eight-hour workshop, actually plan out a six-hour workshop, and then add a third of six, which is another two hours. This usually guarantees that you will cover what you planned to cover, that you don't end up all rushed, and that you can actually give twenty-five minute coffee breaks, which is what they'll end up being anyway.

BALANCE TASK AND PROCESS ORIENTATION

There is considerable talk in adult education circles about task and process orientation. Basically, task in the case of an AFB workshop is accomplishing the objectives of the workshop. Process is the way things are done, the relationships formed between people in the workshop, and the participatory aspect. You can always appear to cover more ground by concentrating on task. But if you don't respect process, then you'll likely only cover ground with a few people.

For example, take the principle of small group work. Lecturing to twenty people allows you to cover a lot of material but you're really only reaching four or five people who learn well that way. If you break them up into four groups of five and have them discuss material with a little guidance or do an activity based on the material, you end up with four people talking and sixteen others listening and interrupting in each group and a much higher involvement in learning. But this kind of process takes time. You must break into groups, repeat instructions, and then understand that probably a lot of what happens in the small group will actually be off-task—people won't be doing precisely what you told them to do. Perhaps they're supposed to analyze a family budget but instead, they continue talking about Adam Smith and Milton Friedman and globalization. This is okay from a process point of view, because they're learning what they want to learn at this point, but it's terrible from a task point of view, because the clock is ticking and you've got all this material to cover.

This workshop has been designed with an even split between task and process, large group discussions and then small group activities or exercises. There is often a temptation to cut down activities and lengthen discussions. If you only have a few hours (not two days), the tendency will be to cut out the activities, especially the introductory activity. This might be okay if you're making a presentation to a board or a group that has already formed, but that's not really a workshop.

Having 50 percent discussion and 50 percent activity is not a rule written in stone, but it is a good average to aim for in any workshop. If you constantly come back and focus on the workshop objectives, you'll have good task orientation.

OBJECTIVES FOR THE WORKSHOP

We have suggested four objectives for the workshop:

1. Basic economic literacy
2. Critique of the values that are now creating budgets
3. Understanding the Alternative Federal Budget
4. A chance to come up with alternatives of your own

Regardless of the objectives you have as a facilitator, you must acknowledge those of the participants. To accomplish your task, when you design and choose activities for your workshop, you should constantly come back to asking the following questions, or to some combination of these and objectives of your own choosing:

1. How can this develop basic economic literacy?
2. How can this critique the values now creating budgets?
3. How can this develop understanding of the AFB? Of job creation? Of alleviating poverty? Of social programs? Of fair taxation? Of managing the debt?
4. How can this give participants a chance to express alternatives of their own?
5. How can this meet the stated goals of participants?

Finally, remember that budgets are about politics, and that good democratic politics works best with participation from everyone. That's what we want from our workshop, and what we hope for in future budgets—official or alternative. That's what this book is for.

2. Budget Basics: Introducing Alternative Budgets

A budget is a plan or an estimate for the spending and income for the coming year. It can be for a family, a business, or a government. The main categories in a budget are:

Revenue

The income that is expected in the coming year.

Expenditure

The amount of spending that is likely to take place in the coming year.

Surplus / Deficit

The difference between revenue and expenditure. If there is money left over, there is a surplus. If expenses exceed revenue, there is a deficit.

Debt / Assets

The total value of the organization. If there was a deficit this becomes part of the debt. Assets refer to those items of worth which the organization owns and could sell.

Debt Servicing Charges

If there is a debt, interest must be paid on the debt. Making these payments is called servicing the debt. Many lenders do not care if the debt is ever paid as long as you continue to make your interest payments.

What does all of this look like in a federal budget? The following table gives the Canadian government's 1998-99 figures for spending, revenue, and the operating balance. In the first exercise, we are going to ask you to guess what some of the other numbers are. Here is what the 1998 federal budget looked like:

This discussion and the exercise that follows are designed to provide a brief, fun activity that allows people to get to know one another in a non-threatening way, as well as learn some budget basics. The discussion should take about ten minutes, and the exercise twenty minutes.

Review the key components of a budget, explaining their relationship to one another. The first thing to explain is—what is a budget?

We have put a few numbers in here to help people get their bearings for "The Price is Right" exercise, and you are going to start by asking them to try to fill in a few blanks.

Explain to participants that over the course of the workshop, no one is going to explain what every budget line means. Point out that many people who are quite knowledgeable about budgets generally find themselves guessing when they are asked to explain what particular expenditures are. When this exercise is done by people who are very familiar with the AFB, most of them usually have no idea what the correct numbers are for the blank spaces. The numbers change from year to year and have to be revised throughout the year.

The 1998-99 Federal Budget

(All figures in billions of dollars.)

REVENUE

Personal Income Tax
Corporate Income Tax
EI Premiums
GST
Excise Taxes
Other Revenue

TOTAL REVENUE   151.0

EXPENDITURES

Old Age Security
EI Payments
Transfers to Governments
Other Transfers
Transfers to Crown Corps
Defence
Government Operations

TOTAL PROGRAM SPENDING   104.5

OPERATING BALANCE   46.5

PUBLIC DEBT CHARGES

TOTAL EXPENDITURES

SURPLUS / (DEFICIT)

NET PUBLIC DEBT

Exercise 1:
The Price is Right

Now, try to guess the figures for the following six budget lines in the 1998-99 federal budget, as prepared by Finance Minister Paul Martin. Refer to the table on the previous page for help. Martin's figures are given on the next page. Interestingly, those figures are only estimates—we won't find out what really happened until February, 1999. For now, though, it's interesting to note that most AFB economists predict that his figures underestimate the operating balance. This suggests a much smaller deficit or even a surplus.

1. Personal Income Tax

The amount of money the government expects to receive from taxing individuals.

2. Corporate Income Tax

The amount of money the government expects to receive from taxing corporations.

3. Public Debt Charges

The amount of money the government expects to pay on the money it owes.

4. Surplus / Deficit

The expected difference between government revenues and government expenditures.

5. Net Public Debt

The total amount of money that the government owes. Deficits from previous years added together make up the total debt.

PRICE IS RIGHT: 1998 FIGURES

(All figures in billions of dollars.)

1. Personal Income Tax	71.0
2. Corporate Income Tax	20.5
3. Public Debt Charges	43.5
4. Surplus / (Deficit)	3.0
5. Net Public Debt	583.2

How did you do? We'll look at the federal budget in more detail later—if you're interested in the other line items, the complete figures for 1998 can be found at the beginning of chapter 5.

3. How We Got Here: A Layperson's History of Economics

This book is about alternatives to the current federal budget, which means it has something to do with economics, which is often referred to as the "dismal science." And there is going to be a fair bit of economics. But economics is not a science. It has to do with power and change as much as with adding and multiplying. The people who have proposed the Alternative Federal Budget in the past have not done so because they believed that they are better with numbers than the finance minister and his advisers. They have done so because they believe that they have different values. And those values determine their approach to economic ideas. Ideas are important. In the world of economics there are many differing and conflicting ideas. However, at any one given time there is usually one set of ideas that dominates the age—that is seen as the "common sense" of the era. Understanding that the "common sense" of one's own time was once seen as ridiculous or impractical can be liberating. It allows you to realize that just as the dominant ideas of the past have come and gone, the dominant ideas of the present will one day pass away. It also means that we can play a role in shaping the dominant ideas of the future: indeed if we don't, someone else will. So it is best to start with a snapshot of some economists and their ideas. It is worth noting that all of these economists were men, three of them lived and worked and Europe, while one worked in the United States. We have not picked them because they are our favourite economists, but because for better or worse they have shaped ideas which dominate the world we live in.

Before we begin we should note that this discussion leaves out far more than it includes. For example, there is no mention of the exploitative relationship between the First World and the Third World. You should consider this and other issues not touched upon in this section, to see how they might fit into your own ideas about economics and alternative budgets.

Adam Smith

In his book *The Wealth of Nations*, published in 1776 just as the industrial revolution was getting underway, economist Adam Smith laid the groundwork for what is termed laissez-faire economics. Laissez-faire is simply French for "let it be." Which is what Smith wanted government to do. His ideas are often referred to as classical economics.

Smith asked one central question: How, in an increasingly complex and global society, in which people are increasingly dependent on the actions of others for their survival, can the economic activities of independent producers, shippers, merchants, and consumers be best coordinated? His answer was simple. He said there was no need for coordination. Left to themselves, competitive markets would create order, not disorder. Trouble would only arise if a market was monopolized. He went on to argue that if every member of society simply pursued his or her economic self-interest, all of society would benefit. This was the work of what he called "the invisible hand" of the market that was turning acts of individual greed into public benefit. As Smith put it, "It is not from the benevolence of the butcher, the brewer, or the baker that we expect our dinner but from their regard to their self-interest."

Smith's ideas ruled economic thinking in Canada up until the 1940s.

Canadian Political Economy

1497	1776	1800	1850
John Cabot puts his foot somewhere in North America and claims Newfoundland for England. Affected Indian Nations not consulted (1497)	Adam Smith's *The Wealth of Nations* advocates for laissez-faire economics (1776). Along with Smith, the main classical economists are David Ricardo (1772 –1823), James Mill (1773 – 1836), John Stuart Mill (1806 – 1873)	Publication of the *Communist Manifesto* by Karl Marx (1848) Genocide of Beothuk Nation completed in Newfoundland (1829)	Louis Riel hanged in Regina (1884) Totonto printers win 9-hour day (1872)
		Voyageurs hold first known strike in Canada (1794)	
Jaques Cartier takes a walk in the Gaspé and claims the northern part of the continent for France. Affected Indian Nations not consulted (1534)	Royal Proclamation issued recognizing Indian rights to land and requiring a treaty with the Crown before Indian Nations can be disposessed of their land (1763)		Trade Union Act decriminalizes worker's associations and gives implicit right to strike (1872)

Karl Marx

Karl Marx, who lived in Europe in the middle of the nineteenth century, identified the existence of conflict in economic life. He pointed out that just because two parties reach agreement, they are not both benefiting equally. In other words, the amount of power you have going into a negotiation influences its outcome.

Marx believed that western societies were made up of classes which act to defend and advance their interests. The two central classes in a modern economy he argued were the workers and the employers, who were in conflict with one another. He thought that economic systems were constantly evolving as a result of this conflict. Marx encourages us to ask who is on top and who benefits from economic policy. Marx's ideas have never dominated Canadian economic thinking, but they provide a useful set of questions to ask about economic activities, since he reminds us to ask who gains and who loses. Perhaps the most important thing for us to remember about Marx is that he argued that the goal of intellectual work such as his was to change the world. This focus has led to a rich political legacy.

The Age of Catastrophe: 1900 – 1945 / Laissez-Faire Economics

1900	1935	1940	1945

Northern Québec given to the province of Québec and Northern Ontario given to Ontario. Affected Indian Nations not consulted (1912)

The Great Depression (1929 – 1935)

John Maynard Keynes (1883 – 1946) *The General Theory of Employment, Interest, and Money* (1936)

Family Allowance Act (1944)

Communist Party of Canada founded (1921)

Cooperative Commonwealth Federation (CCF) founded (1932)

Canadian Women win "Person's Case" (1929)

World's financial élite assemble in Breton Woods to establish the World Bank and International Monetary Fund (1944)

Thetford asbestos miners strike (1915)

Women win right to vote (1918)

Jobless occupy Vanouver Post Office (1938)

Montréal garment workers strike (1912)

Picketing decriminalized (1934)

Unemployment Insurance Act (1940)

Winnipeg General Strike (1919)

Public Service strike in Montréal (1943)

Socialist Party of Canada founded (1904)

Québec women win the right to vote (1940)

John Maynard Keynes

John Maynard Keynes, a British economist of the middle twentieth century, attacked then prevailing ideas about unemployment. Laissez-faire economists had argued that unemployment was largely voluntary. If the unemployed dropped their wage demands to a low enough level they would be able to find work. Keynes argued that unemployment is often caused because there is not enough demand for goods. In other words, the way to reduce unemployment might be to raise wages, allowing workers to buy more goods. There is a radical conclusion to this idea: Keynes was arguing that the invisible hand could not cure unemployment, instead it would take the visible hand of government to raise wages. Keynes' ideas formed the basis of government economic policies from the 1940s to the 1970s. The visible hand could spend money on a wide range of goods: it could simply cut corporate taxes, it could build nuclear bombs and bombers, or it could invest in social programs. Keynesianism is associated with the practice of governments running deficits in lean times to balance the economy.

The Golden Age: 1945 – 1975 / Keynesian Economics

1950	1960	1970	1975

Canadian Labour Congress founded (1955)

Health Insurance Act (1970)

General Agreement on Tariffs and Trade (GATT) first signed by 23 nations including Canada (1947)

Canada Pension Plan / Canada Assistance Plan Act (1966)

UN enacts Charter of Economic Rights and Duties of the States (1974)

CCF and CLC form New Democratic Party (1961)

UN signs Universal Declaration of Human Rights (1948)

Minister of Indian Affairs Jean Chrétien releases the 1969 White Paper announcing an intention to end Indian status and assimilate Indian population. Immediately and powerfully rejected by First Nations and subsequently dropped as official policy (1969)

130,000 strike against Canadian National and Canadian Pacific; win 40-hour work week (1950)

Economic Council of Canada founded (1963)

Foreign Investment Review Agency founded (1974)

Fraser Institute founded (1974)

Asbestos miners strike in Québec (1948)

The Watkins Report *Foreign Ownership and the Structure of Canadian Investment* (1968)

CLC holds one day strike against federally imposed wage controls (1976)

Milton Friedman

Milton Friedman is a neo-classical (the name simply means they are giving a slightly new twist to Adam Smith's classic ideas) economist who favoured a return to laissez-faire economics. His idea that un-regulated markets—on a global scale—will produce benefits for all have come to dominate government thinking since the early 1980s. In the 1960s he began calling for an end to government regulation and intervention in the economy (including the end of minimum wage laws and most forms of social security). Neo-classical econo-mists rejected government deficit spending and believed that high rates of unemployment were needed to control wages and inflation. Once the deficit was eliminated and social programs reduced, wages and prices would decline and the economy would grow. The neo-conservatives also believed that government spending was the result of pressure by special interest groups, particularly unions, and there-fore it was necessary to curb their power.

Responses to Neo-classical Economics

The new economic orthodoxy of the market is being challenged by the left. But an alternative to the "common sense" of neo-liberalism

The Landslide: 1975 – Present / Neo-Classical Economics

1980	1985	1990	1995
Courchene Report, *Money, Inflation, and the Bank of Canada*, argues that the Bank of Canada should be fighting inflation (1976)	Canada – US Free Trade Agreement signed by Brian Mulroney and Ronald Reagan (1989)		Negotiations on the Multilateral Agreement on Investment begin at the Organization for Economic Cooperation and Develop-ment (1995)
		CHO!CES: A Coalition for Social Justice is founded (1990)	
Canadian Centre for Policy Alternatives is founded (1980)		North American Free Trade Agreement (NAFTA) (1993)	
Sandra Lovelace takes Canada before the Human Rights Commission of the UN which finds Canada in breach of its international obligation to protect the rights of minorities to participate in their own culture and community (1981)	MacDonald Commission is critical of social programs and calls for decreases in unemployment insurance benefits (1985)	Canada Health and Social Transfer (CHST) amalgamates and decreases the federal tax and cash transfer for social programs (1996)	
		First Alternative Federal Budget launched by CHO!CES / CCPA (1995)	

will have to be more than just a revival of the old Keynesian ideas. In recent years thinkers on the left have pursued ideas and practices that never occurred to Marx.

Left feminist economists critical of neo-liberalism argue that the market is itself gender biased. Markets are as much political and cultural institutions as they are economic ones, and both reflect women's inequality and perpetuate it. Economic restructuring, which has fallen heavily upon women globally, gives a clear illustration of this.

Keynesian policies, such as health care, unemployment insurance, and pensions, have helped to reduce gender inequalities. But feminist economists point out that government policies affect men and women differently. Look at taxation, for instance. Because men earn more than women, they are most affected by changes to income taxes. But as the main managers of household budgets, women are hit harder by sales taxes, which place increased pressure on them to economize on clothing and other purchases. Although the impact of taxes on poorer people is often discussed, the differing effects on women and men are not as clearly understood. Feminist economics suggests ways in which we could plan policy with a greater awareness of its impact upon women's equality.

Feminist economists have also raised basic questions about what we count and what we assign value to in the economy. They have criticized Keynesianism for largely ignoring the unpaid labour of women in caring and reproduction, as well as the contribution of this labour to economic health and human development. Perhaps the most well known is Marilyn Waring, whose book *If Women Counted* has generated popular awareness of the gender bias of mainstream economics.

The exploitation of the environment has led to the growth of green economics. Like feminism, it has questioned what counts as economic growth. It is sobering to realize, for instance, that an enormous environmental disaster which involves an expensive clean up will register as a positive increase in the gross domestic product (an indicator accounting for all the economic activity that takes place in a country). Some have proposed a genuine progress indicator, a way to count economic activity that distinguishes between desirable and undesirable economic activity.

IDEAS IN ACTION: A SHORT ECONOMIC HISTORY OF THE TWENTIETH CENTURY

Good Times, Bad Times

The British historian Eric Hobsbawm has divided the history of our century into three ages. Adam Smith's ideas dominated the first one, which Hobsbawm called the age of catastrophe. The second, our century's brief golden age, was dominated by Keynes, while the current age, the age of the landslide, has been dominated by Friedman. We might say that the ideas of Karl Marx have haunted all three ages, but never dominated them. The following is a brief outline of that history. It should be noted that this history captures the Canadian, not the global experience. And within the Canadian experience there would be many groups and peoples whose experiences run counter to the general experience. Aboriginal peoples for instance were in many ways better off during the period 1900 – 1945 than they were in the period following 1945.

The Age of Catastrophe: 1900-1945

From 1900 to 1945 we experienced two world wars and two worldwide depressions. Economic competition drove nations to war, while a belief that governments should not interfere in the economy prolonged the depressions. In Canada during the 1930s, one out of every four workers was unemployed. During these years:

- There was no national health program—if people could not afford medical care, they were dependent on the doctor's charity
- Welfare was funded by municipalities—communities with high rates of unemployment often offered the lowest levels of relief
- Schools were forced to close, students were charged for their textbooks. Few students finished high school. Only the children of the wealthy went to university
- There was no unemployment insurance. Single unemployed men were paid 25 cents a day to work in remote camps
- Workers could be fired for joining unions

Politicians expressed sympathy for the poor and the unemployed, but they said that high rates of support would only discourage them from looking for work and rob them of their work ethic. Finally, it was believed that nothing that governments could do would create jobs. Keynes had written his major works by this period, but they had little impact. As economist Paul Samuelson has noted, the economics profession advances funeral by funeral: it was not until the major classical economists had died that Keynes received a hearing.

The Golden Age: 1945-1975

The ideas of the classical economists were discredited by the Second World War. Almost overnight Canada went from having too many workers to having a labour shortage. And the reason was simple: massive government intervention in the economy. Unemployment

This chapter draws on information from Eric Hobsbawm's *The Age of Extremes: The Short Twentieth Century, 1914 – 1991* (Abacus, 1995), and *Understanding Capitalism: Competition, Command, and Change in the U.S. Economy* (Harper Collins, 1993), by Samuel Bowles and Richard Edwards.

was eliminated as men and women joined the armed forces or went to work in the booming war industries. The government was soon controlling wages and prices.

As unemployment disappeared workers became more confident about asserting their rights on the job. In 1943 a record number of strikes took place in Canada. Canadian voters also began to show their support to the left-wing political ideas that had been floating around for the past few decades. In 1943 the Cooperative Commonwealth Federation (the forerunner to the NDP) became the official opposition in Ontario and Québec. People who had seen government intervention end a depression were not prepared to return to the days of laissez-faire economics when the war ended.

It was to end the waves of strikes and to stop the growing support for both the CCF and the Communist Party that the Liberals committed themselves to Keynesianism in the final years of the war.

The first of the modern social programs, the family allowance, was introduced in 1944. In the following years workers were given the legal right to strike while employers were compelled to bargain with certified unions. Unemployment insurance, the Canada Pension Plan, medicare, and a national set of standards for welfare known as the Canada Assistance Plan were all introduced in the twenty years following the war.

These were the golden years, when unionized wages allowed thousands of families to greatly increase their standard of living while government programs increased their sense of security.

The government also committed itself to maintaining close to full employment by using its spending and taxing powers to increase demand. Government spending created employment by building schools, hospitals, and senior citizens residences, and hiring people to work in these institutions. It created jobs by spending millions on weapons research and purchases. Tax cuts stimulated investment and consumption. When there was a bust in the economy, consumption was sustained because unemployed workers received unemployment insurance and were not driven into bankruptcy by unexpected medical bills. This period is sometimes referred to as the era of the postwar labour accord, when large business agreed to deal with unions, while unions were able to improve living standards out of an increasingly productive economy.

But to use an idea of Marx's, conflicts between the main classes in a society drive that society's history. The labour accord did not last forever. Many of the elements that created this golden age contributed to its coming into crisis in the late 1960s and early 1970s. Secure and increasingly well-educated workers took advantage of their bargaining position—in the 1960s there was another massive wave of strikes. At the same time, corporations came under increasing public scrutiny and criticism. Scandals surrounding pollution, price gouging, and bribery undermined corporate legitimacy. In 1972 NDP leader David Lewis captured the public imagination with a campaign that attacked the corporate welfare bums. At the same time events such as the American defeat in Vietnam and the Watergate scandal brought governmental authority into disrepute. Finally, corporate profits, assaulted both by workers at home and by foreign competition, were declining. The 1970s brought a new phenomenon not encompassed in Keynesian thought—stagflation: high inflation and rising unemployment at the same time. For workers and for employers, Keynesianism was no longer delivering the goods.

A new round in the war of ideas was about to be fought: this time however, the business community was to get its act together and win a decisive victory.

The Landslide: 1975 to the Present

The 1970s were a period of extended conflict and turmoil. Governments began abandoning many of the elements of the postwar labour accord: for example, freezing wages and legislating ends to strikes.

It was during this period that leading corporate figures in Canada and around the world began searching for a new set of economic ideas. Secondly, they sought to counter the poor public image that corporations had developed in the previous decade. The Trilateral Commission, a think-tank that included representatives from leading corporations and governments in western Europe, North America, and Japan, published a report which concluded that the West was suffering from an excess of democracy. The public sector was too large, the universities and media were too critical, unions were too aggressive, and education was no longer matched with employment needs. Milton Friedman's ideas provided a near perfect solution for these problems.

Canadian corporations bankrolled a number of organizations in the 1970s which began to make the argument for neo-classical or neo-conservative (or, as they are sometimes called, neo-liberal) ideas. Economist Michael Walker was recruited from the Bank of Canada to head the corporate-funded Fraser Institute. Walker said, "If you really want to change the world, you have to change the ideological fabric of the world." The Fraser Institute was soon publishing books, studies and leaflets outlining the dangers of big government, big unions, and social programs. In a slightly more low-key fashion the corporate-sponsored C.D. Howe Institute published an ongoing series of reports which highlighted the dangers of government deficits and the need to make Canadian labour more competitive.

The message to Canadian people was simple and direct: the Canadian government was living beyond its means. A common message was if households operated with the sorts of debt and deficits the government did they would soon go broke.

By the 1980s the neo-classical economists had won the war of ideas. They held office in London, Ottawa, and Washington. Their policies involved:

If you're doing the full workshop, you should be just over half way through the first morning by now—time for a break, maybe, before you finish off the morning with chapter 4.

- High interest rates that kept unemployment high

- Restrictions on trade union rights such as legislating ends to strikes, passing laws making it harder to organize, and not prosecuting anti-union employers

- Shifting the tax burden from high income earners and corporations to consumers

- Drastically reducing the size of the public sector and reducing the range and scope of social programming

The results of these policies include increases in poverty, a twenty year decline in living standards, chronic unemployment, and what has been termed jobless growth.

The authors of these policies often acknowledge that they are strong medicine, but argue that they are necessary short term pain to set the stage for long term gain. Once government is cleared out of the way, once workers are prepared to be realistic in their wage demands, they argue, job creation will surge forward. Even if it doesn't, there is no alternative.

These arguments have not been accepted passively. Trade unions, social movements, and progressive political parties have consistently opposed neo-conservative policies and have developed alternatives to them, of which the AFB is one. This opposition has led to the establishment of progressive institutions, including alternative think-tanks such as the CCPA, to counter right-wing ideologies and policies.

The claim that "there is no alternative" is often referred to the as the TINA syndrome. As this admittedly crude history suggests, however, there are always alternatives. Those who oppose the current dominant ideas have two responsibilities. The first is to challenge the pain that is being inflicted on millions of Canadians through policies which create and deepen poverty and unemployment. The second is to create a new set of ideas that may become the "common sense" of a future era.

The real value of any Alternative Federal Budget is that it is a process in which people with ideas quite different from those of the status quo can prove that there are alternatives. What different ways can we go forward—or does it even make sense to speak of something called forward?

4. Looking at a Family Budget

Despite some problems of simplification, we think a good place for us to start thinking about budgeting as a reflection of our values and politics is by looking at the simple common family budget, so often used as an example by neo-conservatives. There are a lot of ways in which family and federal budgets cannot be compared—an important political issue that we'll be discussing shortly—but in order to understand general budgetary terms, we feel it's a good starting point.

To really understand a budget, you have to hold it in your hands and crunch the numbers, seeing how one set of figures affects others. For instance, people often speak of there being two separate sides to a budget—the revenue side, which lists all the expected income and its sources; and the expenditure side, which outlines where one plans to spend this money.

The totals do not have to be equal. If revenue decreases, we usually cut expenses somewhere. If revenue is greater than expenditures, then the budget is said to be in surplus and we can squirrel money away for our old age. If expenditures are greater than revenue the budget is in a deficit situation.

Surpluses turn into assets that governments can use to create a variety of rainy day funds. For example, in the 1970s when oil revenues were high, the Alberta government set up a Heritage Fund. In a family budget, the major asset is usually a house.

Deficits are added to the debt. It is not necessary to pay off debts. Often, they are balanced by the assets (that's what a balance sheet is about). However, debts must be serviced, which means that it is necessary to make interest payments on your debts. For this reason, if there is a debt, debt-servicing will be an expense to be entered as an expenditure.

Workshop participants should form groups of three to six people. After the small group session, discuss the questions as a large group.

This exercise is fairly straightforward and gives people a first experience of working with a budget. In a familiar context (a family budget), participants learn and apply the skill of teasing out the numbers and consider how the choices made affect family life. The exercise encourages us to ask, "What is important here: the numbers (read economics), or the family?" When we get to the government budgets, we'll be asking a similar question: "What is important: economics or people?" This exercise starts us thinking about the approach of measuring three factors—choices, impacts, and values—as a way to analyze budgets and answer these important questions.

Exercise 2: Budget for a Family Emergency

We said that the best way to get to know a budget is by working with it, crunching the numbers. On the following page, we've reproduced a budget for a mythical Canadian family—two parents, both working to pay off their $75,000 home, three children at home, a grandmother in a nursing home and the need to supplement the income of a brother (uncle) with disabilities. The budget shown here is their 1998 budget.

We have given this family a comfortable income and a house. This isn't because we think this represents the way "average" or "normal" families live. We have done this because it provides the family with a measure of economic flexibility. The exercise will demonstrate the different ways a family might exercise this flexibility in the face of a family crisis.

Near the end of 1998 there is a family crisis. The eight year old son, Martin, has been diagnosed with a learning disorder. The public school system is not funded to deal with the problem—as a result he is falling behind in school and coming into increasing conflict with teachers and his peers. The family has a chance to enrol him in 1999 in a special tutoring program that has had considerable success in helping students like him stay in school. The one year program costs $10,000.

There are a number of ways that the family can respond. Whatever the response, it will reflect the family's underlying values. The table "Three Budgets for a Family Emergency" shows three different responses. By comparing the 1998 budget with the three 1999 budgets, try to figure out what the family did in each case, and perhaps why they did it.

A word of warning: there are no right or wrong answers in this exercise. Budgets do not necessarily give us all the information we need. The purpose of this exercise is to give you experience in teasing out information about underlying values from budgets. These figures are only rough estimates, so keep your eye on the big picture.

Try to answer three questions about budgets A, B, and C. What are the choices that the family has made? What will the impacts of these choices be? What values does this budget represent?

Family's 1998 Budget

(All figures in thousands of dollars.)

REVENUE

Father's Salary	50
Mother's Salary	25
TOTAL INCOME	**75**

EXPENDITURES

Basic Family Costs:	
Food	12
Taxes	20
Clothing	3
Transportation	3
Utilities, Maintenance	5
Other (Insurance, Charity	
Entertainment, Pet)	6
Individual Costs:	
Michael's (3) Daycare	3
Martin's (8) Allowance	1
Mary's (17) Allowance	2
Mother's Nursing Home	5
Disabled Brother	
(Supplement Welfare)	3
TOTAL EXPENDITURE	**63**

Operating Balance	12
Debt Payments:	
Mortgage Interest	6
Mortgage Principal	6

Surplus / (Deficit)	0

Assets / (Debt)	
Mortgage Owed	(25)
Home	75

After the family budget exercise, discuss with the participants some of the differences between budgeting for a family and budgeting for a government.

The point of this exercise is to begin to use the skills and information we've learned to this point to analyze budgets and to generate some interesting discussion, so there are no "correct" answers to the questions. However, here are some possible interpretations: In "A" the family has sold the home, which allows them to pay for the program and stay out of debt. In "B" they have done nothing. In "C" the family has chosen to borrow money to renovate the basement, which has provided it with an additional revenue stream. Again, the most important thing to come out of this exercise should be a recognition that budgetary decisions reflect the values of the people who make them.

Three Budgets for a Family Emergency

	A	B	C
Father's Salary	50	50	50
Mother's Salary	25	25	25
Rent Room			4
Sale of House	50		
TOTAL INCOME	125	75	79
EXPENDITURES			
Basic Family Costs:			
Rent	7	0	0
Food	9	12	11
Taxes	20	20	20
Clothing	3	3	3
Transportation	3	3	3
Utilities, Maintenance	5	5	7
Other (Insurance, Charity Entertainment, Pet)	6	6	5
Individual Costs:			
Michael's (3) Daycare	3	3	3
Martin's Program	10		10
Martin's (8) Allowance	1	1	1
Mary's (17) Allowance	2	2	2
Mother's Nursing Home	5	5	5
Disabled Brother (Supplement Welfare)	3	3	3
TOTAL EXPENDITURE	77	63	73
OPERATING BALANCE	48	12	6
DEBT PAYMENTS			
Bank Loan			6
Mortgage Interest		6	6
Mortgage Principal		6	6
SURPLUS / (DEFICIT)	48	0	(12)
ASSETS / (DEBT)			
Mortgage Owed	0	(19)	(19)
Home	0	77	77
Savings	48		
Bank Loan			(7)

Differences Between Federal and Family Budgets

Family and federal budgets look the same. They have revenue, expenditure, deficits or surpluses, debts or savings. But there are a number of important differences.

1. Governments Have Much More Control Over Both Revenue and Expenditures

Most Canadian households get their income from employment revenue. (Many wealthier families also get income from investments.) It is difficult to significantly increase revenue from one year to the next unless another family member is put out to work or a family member dramatically increases the number of hours he or she works. In short, families have little flexibility over revenue. The changes they can make usually take place on the expenditure side. This is why when people transfer their thoughts from household budgets to federal budgets, they usually start looking for where to cut spending, not increase revenue. Governments can increase their revenue by increasing taxes, raising fees, selling off assets, and developing new revenue streams (gambling, for instance).

2. Governments Can Print Money

If families allow their debt to grow beyond their ability to make payments, the family can go bankrupt. Governments, because they have the ability to print money, cannot go bankrupt in this sense since they do not run out of money to pay their debts. Printing endless amounts of money can cause inflation and make it very difficult to pay for goods that are being imported into the country, however.

3. Household Debt is Debt Owed to Outsiders, While a National Debt is Usually Owed to Other Canadians

If one family member borrows money from another family member, the overall household economy is not weakened, although family income has been redistributed. It is only when loans are made with outside agencies such as banks or credit unions that debt becomes a burden. The bulk of the national debt in Canada is raised from the sale of bonds to Canadian citizens. In this sense the national debt resembles an internal household debt. It is only when the debt is held outside the country that the interest payments became a drain on the country's wealth.

4. Government Budgets Ignore the Government's Own Assets

Much of the government debt should be set against the hospitals, schools, roads, and other physical assets which were constructed by government and which generate wealth, taxes, and employment income, and support the generation of wealth, taxes, and employment. Knowing that a family has a $50,000 debt does not tell us much about that family's financial position until we find out if that debt is the mortgage on their $75,000 home or their outstanding Diner's Club bill. The fact that government assets are not fully considered when we determine assets is a political decision—and we should ask whose interests it serves.

In fact, many of these differences between federal and family budgets are politically significant. It's no coincidence that right-wing economists and commentators rely so heavily on the idea that a family budget and a government budget are the same; if you accept that notion, you'll only naturally feel the government should cut spending rather than raise revenues. Neo-conservatives often argue that, "No family would operate the way the government does." What they rarely mention is that to do so would be absurd.

5. Values in a Government Budget

Let's look at a real, if simplified, version of the federal budget. This is the budget more or less as it appears in the document that the federal government publishes when the budget is released. That is, it is nothing magical—and the concepts we learned in the last chapters can be applied here.

Now participants get into their hands a real federal budget, and there's a fair amount of room for line-by-line discussion. This discussion could take half an hour or several hours, depending on how detailed you and the participants want to get.

In our experience, somewhere around half an hour is best, because, even though you can go on and on, the idea at this point is simply to get familiar with the categories of a budget.

If you're doing a full two-day workshop, you should now be beginning the first afternoon. This chapter should take not much more than an hour in total.

The Martin Budget 1998-99

(All numbers are in billions of dollars.)

REVENUE

Personal Income Tax	71.0
Corporate Income Tax	20.5
EI Premiums	18.6
GST	20.9
Customs and Excise Taxes	11.1
Other Revenue	8.9
TOTAL REVENUE	**151.0**

EXPENDITURE

Old Age Security	22.9
EI Payments	12.6
Transfers to Governments	19.5
Direct Program Spending	17.0
Transfers to Crown Corps	3.8
Defence	7.9
Other	20.8
TOTAL PROGRAM SPENDING	**104.5**
Operating Balance	46.5
Public Debt Charges	43.5
Total Expenditures	148.0
Surplus / (Deficit)	3.0
Net Public Debt	583.2

Let's go through the Martin budget line by line.

REVENUE

Personal Income Tax

The first line shows us that the major source of government revenue in Canada is the personal income tax. In Canada the income tax system is supposed to be progressive. The more you make, the higher your rate of taxation.

Corporate Tax

The amount that corporate taxes contribute to the federal revenue has been declining. In the mid 1980s it accounted for 15 percent of government revenue. By 1993, it was down to 7.5 percent.

Employment Insurance Premiums

These are the premiums that workers and employers pay into the employment insurance fund. If you look on the expenditure side you will see that the government was planning to collect far more than it intends to spend on EI.

The Goods and Services Tax

This consumption tax, which was brought in by the Mulroney government, has not been abolished by the Chrétien Liberals. When you see how much money it brings in, you can see why. Critics of this tax point out that it falls on everyone when they make a purchase, regardless of their ability to pay.

Excise Taxes and Other Revenue

For our purposes here we will ignore excise taxes, which are taxes on imports; and other revenues, which are likely to include a wide range of matters such as fees and the income generated by the sale of Crown corporations.

EXPENDITURES

Old Age Security

These are payments made to senior citizens. They come in the form of the old age security payment and the Guaranteed Income Supplement. The Canada Pension Plan does not show up in the government budget either as an expense or a revenue item since it is supposed to be a self-financing system.

EI Payments

EI payments are the payments made to people who are receiving employment insurance. Martin has also drastically cut the amount that is paid out in employment insurance benefits. Fewer than 55 percent of the unemployed are now eligible for employment insurance and the rates have been dropped to the level that were paid in the 1950s.

Transfers to Governments

This budget line includes some of the government's most significant spending such as funding to provincial governments for health, post-secondary education, welfare, and equalization.

Since 1993 the Chrétien Liberals have enacted a number of sweeping changes to Canada's social programs. The most significant has been the creation of the Canada Health and Social Transfer (CHST). This new transfer payment to the provincial governments provides them with funding for health, post-secondary education, and social assistance. It represents a major shift from the way those programs had been funded in the past. Previously, there had been separate funding arrangements for health, post-secondary education, and social assistance. In the case of social assistance and health care there were national standards. There were requirements that the provinces not use money received from the federal government for those two programs in other areas. The CHST has changed all this. It is a block grant to the provinces. If a provincial government so desires it can use CHST money to build roads.

Under the previous Canada Assistance Plan, provincial governments were required to provide welfare to anyone in need—that requirement is no longer in effect. There is only one federally imposed standard on social assistance—provincial governments cannot put residency requirements on social assistance. This law has had the effect of lowering welfare rates across the country. When one government lowers the rate, social assistance recipients may consider moving to a province with a higher rate. The province with the highest rates cannot protect itself from an influx of social assistance recipients who are being driven out of their home province unless it too lowers it rates. The CHST also opened the door for provincial governments to impose workfare requirements, which have the impact of forcing down local wage rates.

The former social assistance funding formula also worked to stabilize the economy during a recession. It did so through a requirement that Ottawa match the amount that the provinces spent on social assistance. During a recession, for example, more people go on social assistance. Therefore provinces end up spending more on social assistance. Under the old system, the federal government would pick up half of the increased costs, which had the effect of taking some of the sting out of recessions, since provinces were not forced to lower their welfare rates to deal with the large number of social service recipients. Now the provinces will have to pick up the additional costs on their own during a recession.

While medicare standards remain in place, the federal govern-

This section (and most of the workshop) is an example of sequential learning. The first step was crunching numbers in a familiar setting. Now, participants are getting used to the way numbers are set up in a federal budget. In the "The Martin Budget and Two Alternatives" exercise, which follows, they crunch numbers in this new setting, using the choices, impacts, values method, and they reach conclusions about economic values relating back to the earlier section on economic history. Give them time in the small group activity to discuss the philosophy of the two alternatives in the context of this history and to consolidate all of the learning that's happening.

By the end of this section, participants have covered a lot of ground. It might be a good time for a chance to reflect, perhaps going around the circle to ask how people are doing, whether they're getting what they need, what they're looking for?

ment has lost much of its power to enforce these standards. That is because the Liberals have also been cutting the amount of money that is spent on health care. In fact, the Liberals had to bring in the CHST because they recognized that they could not force the provinces to live up to the old rules at the same time that Ottawa was cutting provincial transfers.

Direct Program Spending

This is spending through government programs, such as agricultural subsidies, aboriginal health, industrial and regional development programs, international aid, and so on. It also includes programs such as fisheries, broadcasting, aviation, Revenue Canada, and the coast guard, where federal monies do add to provincial economies and provide (mostly unionized) jobs.

Transfers to Crown Corporations

This includes funding to Crown corporations such as the Canadian Broadcasting Corporation, and Atomic Energy of Canada, Ltd.

Defence

This is funding for the Canadian Armed Forces.

Other

This category covers the operating costs of most government departments and funds centrally administered.

Surplus / Deficit and Remaining Line Items

The conservative victory of the last twenty years has been to enshrine the belief that overly generous spending on social programs has caused the debt and the deficit to rise to dangerous levels. These two beliefs—that debts and deficits are too high and that they were created by social spending—have been the driving forces behind the right's takeover of public discourse in Canada. As we discuss below, it is now common knowledge that in fact the current large deficits were created by the high interest rate / low inflation policies of the Mulroney years, not by social spending. In the 1998-99 Martin budget there was a surplus—despite this fact, cuts to expenditures continued.

Exercise 3: The Martin Budget and Two Alternatives

The table below shows the 1998-99 Martin budget and two other possible versions, which reflect different choices for the same budget. Go over them line by line to be sure you understand them. Then compare the three.

Unlike the family budget exercise, this exercise presents alternate budgets for the same year as the first budget, rather than for the following year. As in the family budget exercise, identify what is going on. See if you can identify the choices that have been made and the economic thinkers you would associate with budgets A and B. What are some of the main choices that have been made? What impact will these choices have on Canadians? What values do these budgets represent?

The Martin Budget
and Two Alternatives

(All figures are in billions of dollars.)

	MARTIN	A	B
REVENUE			
Personal Income Tax	71.0	69.0	71.0
Corporate Income Tax	20.5	18.0	31.0
EI Premiums	18.6	17.0	18.0
GST	20.9	23.0	20.0
Excise Taxes	11.1	11.0	11.0
Other Revenue	8.9	9.0	9.0
Total Revenue	151.0	147.0	160.0
EXPENDITURES			
Old Age Security	22.9	21.0	24.0
EI Payments	12.6	13.0	15.0
Transfers to Governments	19.5	18.0	31.0
Direct Program Spending	17.0	18.0	17.0
Crown Corps	3.8	4.0	4.0
Defence	7.9	9.0	10.0
Other	20.8	17.0	19.0
Total Program Spending	104.5	100.0	120.0
Operating Balance	46.5	47.0	40.0
Public Debt Charges	43.5	43.0	41.0
Total Expenditures	148.0	143.0	161.0
Surplus / (Deficit)	3.0	4.0	(1)
Net Public Debt	583.2	580.0	587.0

6. Values in an Alternative Budget

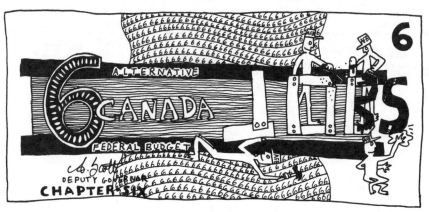

This section deals with what is known as macroeconomic policy. Macroeconomic theory simply means big economic theory. It reflects the idea that governments, through spending and taxing, setting interest rates, and influencing investment, have an impact on the broader economy (for example, unemployment, economic growth, and inflation).

In this section, we begin to discuss macroeconomics and the Alternative Federal Budget, first by talking about job creation.

Allow plenty of time—ideally at least two hours—for this chapter, as it is the most difficult and the exercises are challenging. Schedule a break after exercise 4.

This section attempts to explain why the people who put the Alternative Federal Budget together believe it will achieve a number of important economic goals. Macroeconomics may seem complex. However, the debate is essentially over two main issues. The first is how governments can create jobs and growth. The second is how—or whether—governments can fund job creation and growth policies. This second debate introduces us to conflicts over the size of the debt and the deficit and the tension between inflation and unemployment.

It is important to understand at this point that the Alternative Federal Budget is a budget that attempts to create growth: that is, it attempts to create an economic climate in which more people are put to work producing more goods and services. For many very good reasons some people are increasingly suspicious of the idea of growth. They associate growth with pollution, consumption, and materialism. And these critics have often been correct. However, growth need not be socially and environmentally destructive. To give but one example, housing the homeless could be seen as socially responsible growth. In the expenditure portion of the AFB you will see proposals that give priority to socially beneficial growth.

Aside from the potential social benefits of certain types of growth, increased employment not only helps fight poverty, it can have a positive impact on a government's budget. While it may cost money to create a job, government also can collect taxes from an employed worker and does not have to pay that worker welfare or employment insurance.

CREATING JOBS

In an economy dominated by the private sector, most goods or services are created or provided in order to generate a profit. Producers attempt to produce only enough goods or services to meet demand. When demand increases employers increase production. And to do this they are required to hire more workers.

Therefore one way to increase employment is to increase the demand for goods and services. And there are a number of ways that government can do this.

- Governments can buy more goods and services

- Governments can hire more employees

- Governments can increase minimum wages and the wages that they pay workers. Both of these measures will give workers more money, allowing them to turn needs into demand

- Governments can transfer funds to other agencies and governments and these bodies will hire people and purchase goods and services

- Governments can redistribute wealth from the wealthier members of society to the poorer members of society. This increases demand since low-income individuals spend a larger portion of their income than high income individuals

- Governments can lower interest rates. If interest rates are lower, both consumers and producers are more likely to borrow money. Consumers will use that money to buy goods, employers will use it to expand production. Both measures increase employment

Governments can also protect demand during periods of rising unemployment and economic hardship. It can be done in two ways. Governments can make a decision to increase spending or they can establish policies which automatically put more money into the hands of unemployed people during recessions. These programs are called stabilizers. In Canada, unemployment insurance and the Canada Assistance Plan used to function as stabilizers. As more people qualified for welfare or unemployment insurance, the government simply made payments to these people. This way demand did not fall as far as it would have if these people had not had UI or welfare to rely on.

Exercise 4: How Job Creation Affects Other AFB Goals

The purpose of this exercise is to get participants thinking about how the pieces of the AFB work together. Again, ideally, it should be done in small groups.

The AFB is committed to the following goals:
- Create jobs
- Alleviate poverty
- Maintain and strengthen social programs
- Tax fairly
- Manage the debt

In the following exercise we want you to explore the way that efforts to reach one of these goals can affect—positively or negatively—other goals. Down the left hand column are a number of the macroeconomic job creation measures that we have just discussed. Across the top of the page are the results we are committed to. Write down the ways that you think that each job creation measure might affect, positively and negatively, the other goals. Try to see where these measures would fit together and where they might be working at cross purposes.

	Create Jobs	Poverty Alleviation	Reduce Debt and Deficit	Make Taxation Fairer	Protect Social Services
Government Buys More Goods and Services					
Government Hires More Employees					
Government Redistributes Wealth from Wealthy to Poor					

PAYING FOR JOB CREATION

Debts and Deficits

Government plans to increase demand are even more effective if governments stimulate the economy without increasing taxes, because an increase in taxes reduces demand. (Consumers have to spend their money on taxes, rather than goods and services.)

It is for this reason that governments have engaged in what is called deficit financing. They spend more than they take in. Each year the difference between what they take in and what they spend is added to the national debt. In other words, the existence of a debt and deficit are often crucial elements to a government job creation strategy. Too much debt can drive a family into bankruptcy. While a government cannot go bankrupt, too much debt can lead to a situation where much of the government's revenue is going to pay the interest charges on the debt. When this happens, governments are back where they started from since they are using their tax revenue to pay interest to bankers rather than to stimulate demand.

The best way to look at the budget over time is to consider it as a percentage of the overall economy. At the end of the Second World War the federal government's debt was 120 percent of the gross domestic product (the total value of the goods and services produced in Canada in any given year). That is the largest the debt has ever been in relation to the economy. Yet in the following years the government kept interest rates low, increased social spending, used social programs to redistribute income, and expanded the number of direct government services. The economy grew dramatically and the debt as a percentage of GDP was reduced. In short, the debt and government spending helped kick start the longest boom in Canadian economic history.

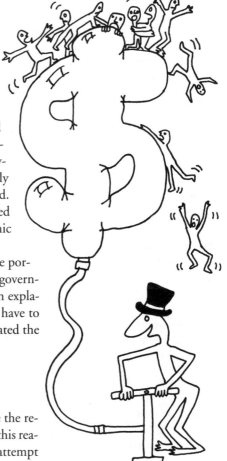

Yet today, the debt is consuming a very large portion of government revenues and reducing the government's ability to set its own agenda. For part of an explanation as to why the 1990s are not the 1940s we have to look at the differences in the way in which we created the debt and the way we fund it.

Creating the Debt—the Danger of High Interest Rates

The common view is that the debt and deficit are the result of excessive spending on social programs. For this reason, politicians can rely on public support if they attempt

Alternative Civic Budgets

Cities and municipalities have several budgets. There are operating, capital, utilities (water, sewer, waste, hydro), and transit budgets. Each municipality sets its own timetable for preparing these budgets, and those preparing an alternative budget will have to become familiar with this timetable.

The operating budget relates to current revenue and expenditure.

Revenues include items like property taxes, business taxes, user fees, fines, transfers from other levels of government, and transfers from utility reserves.

Expenditures include the operating costs for public facilities (libraries, swimming pools, parks, sporting facilities, theatres, museums, zoos) as well as expenditures like road and street maintenance, lighting, policing, fire and ambulance services, administration, and interest on debts the municipality may have accumulated. It is important to note that cities and municipalities are normally required by law to have a balanced operating budget.

The capital budget includes expenditure on the municipality's infrastructure—roads, streets, bridges, buildings. The capital budget is

to ease the country's debt problems by cutting social spending. The AFB rejects the idea that the debt is the product of overspending on social programs. Our belief—and we can point to a number of government and private sector studies to back us up—is that the high debts and deficits Canadians face are in large measure the products of the government's war on inflation which has kept interest rates and unemployment high. Therefore, we believe that the problem can be best addressed by lowering interest rates and reducing unemployment. The best place to start this debate is by looking at the Bank of Canada and its interest rate policies.

The Bank of Canada is a federal agency. It determines interest rates by setting a rate on short-term loans it makes to the chartered banks. Because interest rates are affected by inflation, they can only be compared when they are adjusted for inflation. This adjusted rate is referred to as the real interest rate. Prior to the 1980s the real interest rate charged by the Bank of Canada averaged at 2 percent. Since then the rate has averaged 6 percent. The government has pursued this high interest rate policy as a part of its war on inflation. Unfortunately, this policy has turned into a war on jobs.

Inflation is a general increase in prices. Conservative economists blame inflation on low unemployment. When there is a low rate of unemployment, workers are more secure in their jobs, since they know they can get a new one if they are fired and they know they cannot easily be replaced. For this reason they are more militant and effective in demanding higher wages. And this, some economists argue, leads to inflation.

The Bank of Canada has taken a strong line against inflation. Its main weapon in this battle has been high interest rates. High interest rates are used because they slow the rate of growth in the economy and keep the unemployment rate high. When interest rates are high, employers are not likely to borrow money to invest, workers are not likely to borrow money to make purchases, and as a result, demand goes down. As demand goes down, unemployment goes up. Whenever unemployment starts to fall to a level that the Bank of Canada believes to be inflationary, it raises the interest rates.

In short, strategies to fight inflation are also strategies to create unemployment since low interest rates and low unemployment are seen as causes of inflation.

For employers the war on inflation has one more benefit. It ensures that there is a large number of unemployed people. The existence of this army of unemployed is one of the sticks that an employer uses to get as much productivity as possible out of the workforce. It also means that the employer has to provide workers with fewer carrots.

But how do high interest rates create a large debt and deficit? They do so in two ways. First, increasing unemployment reduces government revenues since unemployed workers don't pay taxes. It also increases government expenses since they do collect EI and social assistance. The result is an increase in both the debt and the deficit. As well, the cost of servicing the debt and deficit is going to be higher since interest payments are higher in a period of high interest rates.

Financing the Deficit

There is one more debate of which you should be aware. This one revolves around the way in which the government finances the deficit. Governments can finance deficits in one of two ways. They can sell bonds or print more money.

Bonds are sold to private purchasers to whom the government must pay interest. The banks are one of the major purchasers of these bonds, although increasingly they are being bought by foreign investors. These investors have a growing influence over Canadian government monetary and fiscal policy.

The Bank of Canada not only sets interest rates, it controls the money supply in Canada—it has the ability to print more money which it can lend to the federal government to cover a portion of the deficit. Since the interest that the government pays on these loans goes back to the government, money raised in this fashion is cheaper than money raised by selling bonds.

During the 1940s the government raised over half the money it needed to cover the deficit by having the Bank of Canada print more money. Today the Bank of Canada covers less than 4 percent of the national debt by printing new money.

The debate here is simple. If the government were to return to its former policy of having the Bank of Canada cover a larger portion of the debt, it would be able to reduce its interest payments since interest payments to the Bank of Canada are simply transfers from one government account to another account. Critics of this policy believe that it would be inflationary, arguing that printing more money brings down the value of existing money. The AFB argues, however, that there would be significant scope for such Bank of Canada purchases before inflation would be affected and, in any case, any expansionary effects could be offset by restricting the lending activities of charter banks.

financed by borrowing.

When there are no "hard" data available, reasonable assumptions should be used to modify what is presented in the municipal government's estimates. If the group putting together the alternative budget feels that a particular department (say, fire) was performing effectively, the decision might be to simply increase spending by the rate of inflation. Detailed work should only be done on parts of the budget where there appear to be major problems.

Once adjustments are made to the government estimates, do a careful scan of the whole budget to ensure coherence between different parts of the budget, and to make sure you haven't lost sight of the forest for the trees: that is, that the budget you end up with reflects the values you wanted it to espouse before you began. This scan is an especially useful step when doing civic budgets, because of the assumptions that sometimes have to be made.

Exercise 5: The Impacts of Different Forms of Financing

This exercise builds on exercise 4. It introduces participants to some more of the complexities in making budgets by getting them to think about and explore the impacts of different ways government might raise revenues.

Take a look at the chart below. Down the left hand column are a number of macroeconomic measures that can be used to finance job creation. Write down the ways that you think that each job creation measure might affect, positively and negatively, the other AFB goals. Try to see where these measures would fit together and where they might be working at cross purposes.

	Create Jobs	Poverty Alleviation	Reduce Debt and Deficit	Make Taxation Fairer	Protect Social Services
Government Lowers Interest Rates					
Government Raises Taxes					
Government Runs a Deficit					
Government Funds Increase out of Growth					
Government Finances Debt by Selling Bonds					
Bank of Canada Finances a Portion of the Deficit					

7. Where We're Going: Meet the AFB

Now we begin to look carefully at the AFB itself, and see how the people who wrote it addressed the same issues and choices that we discussed earlier in the book.

Central Principles

The AFB seeks to adhere to the following principles:

- Job creation should be the government's primary economic concern
- There should be a more equitable distribution of income and wealth in Canada
- There should be economic equality between the sexes and equal treatment of all individuals and families, including all non-traditional families
- The rights of labour must be protected and strengthened
- Protection of the global environment must be strengthened
- The policies advocated for Canadians must not exploit those outside our country
- Public services and social programs play a crucial role in our society and need to be enhanced

Achieving the Goals

Using the above principles as guidelines, the AFB meets the commitments set out in exercise 4, in the following ways:

- Create jobs—This is done through economic policies that stimulate demand, through direct hiring, increasing support for public programs, redistributing working time, and supporting community economic development
- Alleviate poverty—The AFB will not eliminate unemployment, not even over a five year period. Nor will it raise wages to the point where all of the working poor are living above the poverty line. Therefore it is necessary to take additional steps which improve the living conditions of the unemployed, the working poor, and those unable to work

If this is a two day workshop, you're now beginning the second day. People have had a grounding in economics, and we now want to both give them an idea of the content of the AFB, as well as hear their ideas and inputs.

Now that we're beginning to look at the 1998 AFB in detail, participants should ideally have access to a copy of the 1998 Alternative Federal Budget or the *Alternative Budget Papers*, to follow along, both of which are available from Cho!ces and the CCPA.

Alternative Federal Budget Papers 1998

This discussion should be as much about questions as it is about answers. There are many thorny questions in this topic—growth as the target of a budget, mobility of capital, global forces, excess profit taxes. By hearing and respecting diverse opinions, your workshop may come up with new questions and new answers.

• Maintain and strengthen social programs—Federally funded and administered income support, health care, and post-secondary education programs with national standards represent an essential investment in Canada's future. Both funding and standards have been seriously eroded in recent years

• Tax fairly—The AFB seeks to increase government revenue by stimulating growth. But it also proposes ways in which the tax burden could be more equitably shared

• Manage the debt—The AFB accepted the Chrétien government's debt and deficit targets. Not because it accepts the argument that deficits are inherently wrong or that they were caused by excessive social program spending. However, current debt servicing charges and high deficits threaten the security of the other four goals we have established for ourselves

CREATING JOBS

Because we have been speaking about it so much, let's see how the AFB accomplishes its goal of job creation. First, let's review the macroeconomics of job creation. What does the AFB do? The AFB employs all of the previously mentioned methods of increasing employment:

Governments Can Buy More Goods and Services

The AFB increases departmental and program spending. This will require increased direct and indirect public sector spending, particularly on public transit, public infrastructure, retrofitting housing, and building public housing.

Governments Can Hire More Employees

The AFB's $1 billion Infrastructure Program would hire workers to carry out environmental, social, and traditional infrastructure work. Our $1 billion Atmospheric Fund would also employ workers in retrofitting and composting programs.

Government Can Redistribute Wealth

The AFB redistributes wealth in a number of ways. It expands the number of people who are eligible for EI, it cuts middle and low-income taxes, it increases funding for social assistance.

Governments Can Lower Interest Rates

The Bank of Canada would be instructed to ensure that job creation and protecting the government's financial health, along with maintaining price stability, be factored into an interest rate policy. The Bank of Canada would also be instructed to maintain interest rates at 3 – 3.5 percent.

Another means of supporting lower interest rates would be to instruct the Bank of Canada to increase its holdings of the national debt. Over a five year period the bank would acquire up to 10 percent of the debt. This would have the effect of reducing the cost of servicing the debt since the bank is publicly owned.

As interest rates go down, creating jobs and consumer demand, there would be slightly higher inflation. The AFB sets a "target band" for inflation rates of 2 to 4 percent. A low interest rate policy would both stimulate employment growth and reduce debt servicing costs.

In addition to these job creation measures, the AFB suggests ways we can work toward greater democratic control of the economy and create the kind of jobs we need the most. For example, the AFB would introduce programs to support community economic development, and would require banks to reinvest their assets in local economies. We would take steps to reduce working time, both to create jobs and to stop the trend toward longer working hours.

What would all this mean in terms of the actual number of jobs created?

The federal government has predicted that unemployment would be at 8.5 percent in 1999. The AFB would bring it down to 6.9 percent, then to 5 percent in the year 2001. The rate of poverty would fall by 1.5 percent per year.

Before we look at the detailed expenditures and revenue of the Alternative Federal Budget, here is a rough snapshot of the AFB's five year plan:

Measures to Support a "Made in Canada" Interest Rate

• Require commercial banks to reinvest a share of their assets in the communities where they operate

• Phase out the 20 percent allowable foreign investment of tax-subsidized pension and RRSP funds

• Develop alternative financial institutions (such as a National Capital Investment Fund) which keep their money in Canada

• Use the Bank of Canada to refinance 2 percent of the outstanding federal debt per year over the next five years (so that the government pays interest to its own bank, instead of a commercial bank)

• Work internationally towards a Tobin Tax and the establishment of global regulations on international financial flows

AFB's Five Year Plan 1997-2002

(All figures in billions of dollars.)

Fiscal Years	1997 (Forecast)	1998	1999	2000	2001	2002
Revenue	148.2	160.2	167.3	179.0	191.6	205.0
Program Spending	105.8	118.7	127.1	139.7	153.1	167.4
Debt Service Charges	43.8	41.5	39.2	38.4	37.5	36.6
Total Spending	149.6	160.2	166.3	178.0	190.6	204.0
Surplus (Deficit)	**(1.4)**	**0.0**	**1.0**	**1.0**	**1.0**	**1.0**
Net Debt	585	585	584	583	582	581
GDP	849	900	958	1025	1097	1174
Debt as % of GDP	68.9	65.0	60.9	56.8	53.0	49.5

Social Programs

As we begin to consider the spending side of the AFB, let's look at the way it has set about meeting its goals for strengthening and protecting social spending.

Social Investment Funds

The Alternative Federal Budget has taken the destruction of the social safety net as a challenge. We are not proposing that the government simply turn the clock back and restore funding to the previous network of social welfare programs.

The AFB proposes the creation of seven social investment funds. The term social investment fund indicates that these funds support activities which do more than provide a social safety net. Money properly spent on health, education, housing, income support, child care, and unemployment insurance is an investment. Rather than providing a social safety net, these funds will create a measure of social justice.

Central to our concept of social investment funds are appropriate funding formulas and national standards, with provisions made for Québec's autonomy as well as Aboriginal self-government.

The National Health Care Fund

The NHCF will be used to secure a national medicare program based on the five principles of the Canada Health Act: universality; accessibility; portability; comprehensiveness; public administration. To receive federal funding, provinces must adhere to these five principles.

Funding will be stabilized immediately by reversing the cuts made by the Liberal government when they implemented the CHST. In following years health spending will increase as a percentage of growth in the economy.

Special initiatives include legislation to restrict the privatization of health care, the implementation of the Royal Commission on Aboriginal Peoples' health care recommendations, and a national drug plan that would ensure that all Canadians have access to the prescription drugs they need and attack the underlying causes of increases in drug costs.

National Income Support Fund

The Canada Health and Social Transfer abolished the Canada Assistance Plan, the program which set a national standard for social assistance across Canada. The AFB proposes that instead of simply restoring CAP, a National Income Support Fund be established.

The National Income Support Fund would provide a floor of

financial support below which no Canadian's income would be allowed to fall. The floor would initially be set at 60 percent of Statistics Canada's low income cut off level (the poverty line). Over a period of five years it would be increased to 75 percent of this level. Additional funding would also be provided for individuals with special needs, such as those persons with disabilities. Provinces could only gain access to this fund if their income support programs met national standards regarding level of support, appeals procedure, and accessibility.

The fund would support an enhanced child benefit which would not be deducted from provincial social assistance benefits. This fund would initially provide $1,400 per year per child, rising to $1,600 in the second year of our budget. The resources needed to fund the child benefit would fall as the AFB's job creation measures reduce the number of families living in poverty.

Post-Secondary Education Fund

The Post-Secondary Education Fund will set clear national standards and will replace student loans with a system of grants. The national standards will apply to accessibility, comprehensiveness, the transferability of credits, and mobility. Funding for post-secondary education will be restored to its 1995-96 level. In future years funding will increase at a rate determined by the growth of the national economy.

The Child Care Investment Fund

The AFB is proposing the establishment of a federal-provincial Child Care Investment Fund. The fund would provide accessible, affordable, high quality, comprehensive child care programs across Canada.

The Housing Investment Fund

The AFB proposes a renewed social housing program through the establishment of a Housing Investment Fund for the production of non-profit and cooperative housing. The fund would also support a national housing retrofit program.

The Retirement Income Fund

The AFB would use this fund to support the guaranteed income supplement (GIS) and the old age security (OAS) payments. GIS benefits would increase by five percent. The OAS would be indexed to wages rather than prices.

Unemployment Insurance Fund

As a first step to rebuilding the EI system the AFB would expand the scope of individuals covered by EI to 70 percent of the unemployed, over the next four years. This would be done by easing entrance requirements and extending the duration of time a person could receive benefits. Benefit levels would improve to 60 percent of previous insured earnings.

Other Programs

The rest of the AFB's program spending is in federal departments such as Environment, Industry, and Culture. Here is a snapshot of some items that might be of interest:

- $1 billion infrastructure program for public housing, municipal services, environmental cleanup and construction
- $1 billion Atmospheric Fund to support community-based climate change initiatives (retrofitting, transportation, composting, and so on) funded in part by a greenhouse gas fuels tax
- $500 million to support Aboriginal self-government
- $100 million for an equity participation foundation to support organizations working for social and economic equality

You will notice that the table on the following page looks quite different from the Martin budget you were introduced to in chapter 5. It has much more detail about spending, but it also has different line items. Neither of these things is accidental. Early on, the AFB decided to make our budget as transparent as possible, so that anyone looking at our spending can see what our priorities are. To make our budget clear, we combine the figures showing what the AFB would spend in each policy area into a single table. This sounds obvious, but Martin does not present his budget this way. In fact, to find the information about federal spending that we need in order to build our alternative budget each year, we must plough through several government budget documents, make phone calls to government offices, and just generally ask a lot of questions. We need to build the entire picture piece by piece, because government budgets are prepared in a way that makes them largely unintelligible, and the big picture next to invisible.

Some of the figures in our table can be found in the Martin budget—equalization, for example. Others are new. The most important set of numbers in the AFB that you will not see anywhere in Martin's documents is the National Social Investment Funds, because the federal government does not have these funds. So that we can compare apples to apples, the figures for Martin's spending have been reorganized to include the same items as the AFB figures. For example, the budget line Health includes transfer payments for health, the Health Canada budget, and aboriginal health spending. Organizing the figures in this way helps us to see the budget in a new light. The AFB does not lump transfers to provinces into one broad category, as you saw earlier in the Martin budget. The way our table is organized makes spending on social programs clear.

The way we arrive at these figures can be complicated. Because the CHST eliminated separate funding formulas for health, post-secondary education, and income support, we estimate the federal money going to each of these areas. Our estimate is based upon the way funding was allocated between the areas prior to the CHST. So, our table allows you to compare Martin's commitment to these programs with the AFB's commitment. Such a comparison will be the focus of chapter 8, which asks you to analyze the differences between Martin's budget and the AFB.

AFB Program Spending

(All figures in millions of dollars.)

	1997-98 (Martin)	1998-99	1999-2000
NATIONAL SOCIAL INVESTMENT FUNDS			
Health Care Fund	6664	9407	10500
Post Secondary Education Fund	2273	3137	3600
Income Support Fund	5562	7500	8200
Child Care Investment Fund	350	896	1500
Housing Investment Fund	1863	2263	2500
Retirement Fund	22300	23497	24700
Unemployment Insurance Fund	13200	14200	15200
DEPARTMENTAL SPENDING AND OTHER			
Equity Participation Fund	0	100	150
Disabilities-VRDP	168	198	204
First Nations	4308	4808	5308
Common Security (Foreign Affairs and Defence)	13138	12808	12628
Agriculture	1505	1555	1600
Industry (including Infrastructure)	3837	4337	4600
Environment	517	1550	1570
Natural Resources	696	846	981
Fisheries	1077	1127	1161
Transport	1753	1753	1805
Immigration	652	887	913
Human Resources and Training	3544	4195	4321
Justice	3270	3275	3368
Culture	2524	2825	3004
Veterans' Pensions	1921	1840	1840
Equalization	8300	8400	8600
Transfers to Territories	1100	1196	1232
Government Services and Other	5278	6100	7615
TOTAL PROGRAM SPENDING	105 800	118 700	127 100

Exercise 6: Critiquing a Policy Piece

For this exercise, small groups are best, and participants should have some freedom to choose which policy they discuss and the approach they take.

You should plan to take a coffee break after this exercise.

What do you think of the policies we've discussed so far? There are several questions you might ask. First, do they meet the objectives given at the beginning of this section? You might ask, for instance, whether the AFB increases equality between men and women. Or, what would the left feminist economics described at the beginning of this book have to say about our macroeconomic strategies? Our social programs? Or, criticize the budget from an environmental standpoint. How "green" is the AFB? Or, think of what Marx or Keynes (or Friedman) might have to say. Be as critical as you can be!

WHERE WE'RE GOING – HOW TO PAY FOR IT

When we shift to the revenue side of the budget, the bulk of the increase in spending is funded from higher revenues resulting from increased growth in the economy. But the AFB has also identified a number of areas where the tax system contributes to inequalities. Before proceeding to examine the areas that have been identified for reform you should consider the issues that restrict the government's ability to move in this area.

The desire to make the rich pay taxes has to be tempered with the growing mobility of capital. The Canadian tax regime cannot get too far out of line in comparison with that of other industrialized nations. This reality also means that the Canadian government ought to be working toward creating international agreements that protect tax equality across borders. Nonetheless, capital flight is a complex issue, which does not in itself preclude an increase in corporate taxes.

There are other tax inequalities that can be addressed in the federal budget. Let's take a look at the AFB's tax proposals for 1998-99. Indeed, it is the belief of the people who developed the AFB that the other major cause of the country's high debt and deficit is a revenue crisis created by years of tax cuts to high income Canadians and corporations.

CORPORATE TAXES

Closing the Loopholes

There are currently numerous tax breaks available to corporations. These breaks can provide incentives that cause corporations to behave in certain desirable ways and so the AFB does not wish to eliminate these breaks. However, many corporations make use of so many tax breaks that they do not have to pay any tax at all. In Canada over 80,000 profitable corporations paid no tax in 1994. Rather than eliminate all of the various tax deductions, the AFB is imposing a minimum corporate tax which would apply to all profitable corporations. This tax will raise $400 million.

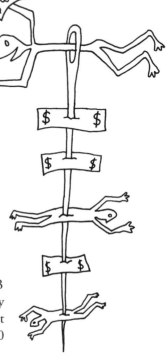

Real Research

The government also issues tax credits for scientific research and experimental development. However, these tax credits have been abused in the past to fund regular corporate operations. The AFB budget would tighten the restrictions on such deductions, and thereby gain an extra $508 million in revenue.

High Salaries

The gap between the salaries corporate leaders make and the wages earned by the men and women who do the work that generates corporate wealth has been increasing dramatically. While the AFB will not put on a limit on the amount that corporations can pay their executives, it will only allow corporations to deduct the first $300,000 of each salary as a business expense. This will raise $50 million.

Meals and Entertainment

Corporations can currently write off 20 percent of the costs of business-related meals and entertainment costs. The AFB proposes the complete elimination of this subsidy of fun and games for the wealthy.

Calling the Tune and Getting Paid for it

Industry invests tens of millions of dollars into lobbying all levels of government. Because businesses are currently allowed to deduct these costs at tax time, the Canadian public ends up paying for $50 million worth of corporate lobbying a year. The AFB would disallow lobbying as a deductible expense.

Taxing the Banks

Every three months it seems the major banks report that their profits have reached new heights. The banks are a federally protected industry and are currently experiencing a rate of profit far higher than other Canadian industries. The AFB is proposing a one-time excess profit tax on the banks that would raise $1.5 billion.

Invest in Canada

Withholding taxes are taxes levied on investors and other nonresidents active in the Canadian economy. These individuals were once taxed at a level comparable to Canadians. However, in recent years that equal treatment has been eliminated. The AFB would increase the withholding taxes to restore equality.

PERSONAL TAXES

The AFB reduces the tax load that low and middle income Canadians carry by approximately $4.3 billion. The 3 percent federal surtax will be eliminated, and the lowest rate of personal income tax will be reduced from 17 percent to 16 percent. The child benefit to low income Canadians will also be increased.

At the same time, the AFB does raise income taxes for high income earners. The top tax rate will increase from 29 percent to 30 percent, and Canadians who make more than $100,000 a year will be taxed at a rate of 33 percent. Those making more than $150,000 will be taxed at a rate of 35 percent.

The AFB would also introduce a tax which would apply to wealth when it is being transferred from one generation to the next. Spouses would be exempt and the tax would not apply to the first million dollars of transferred wealth.

Currently small business owners are exempt from capital gains taxes if the sale of their business earns them less than half a million dollars. In keeping with the AFB's position that all income should be treated equally regardless of source, we are eliminating this exemption.

There are three changes to the GST. The major one increases the size of the rebate to low income Canadians. The second one exempts publications and public transit passes from the tax, while the third change levies the tax on financial transactions, which are currently exempt.

GREEN TAXES

Taxes can also be used as incentives to protect the environment. The AFB is proposing an end to tax breaks that lower the cost of non-renewable energy sources; as it now stands, these are essentially subsidies to the oil and gas industry.

AFB TAX PACKAGE

The following chart shows the way the AFB raises revenue through taxation. For simplicity's sake, we have not included tax relief measures or tax credits like the child benefit. The complete tax package can be found in the budget document.

AFB Tax Revenue

(All figures in millions of dollars.)

TAX EXPENDITURE REFORM

Full Inclusion of Capital Gaims in Income	1180
Eliminate Dividend Tax Credit	640
Integrate Corporate and Personal Tax for Small Business	346

CAPITAL GAINS EXEMPTIONS

Restrict $500,000 Farm Assets Exemption	153
Restrict $500,000 Small Business Exemption	548
Eliminate Capital Gains Freeze, Family Trusts	300

DISALLOWANCE OF CERTAIN DEDUCTIONS

Meals and Entertainment (Corporate and Personal)	305
Lobbying Expenses	50
Salary in Excess of Ten Times Average Wage	50
Restrict Eligibility for Scientific Research Credit	508

INCOME AND WEALTH TAX REFORM

Wealth Transer Tax, Estates over $1,000,000	2925
Increase Top Income Tax Rate from 29 to 30 percent	510
Add New Tax Brackets at $100,000 and $150,000	775

GREEN TAXES

$4 / Tonne Carbon Fuel Tax	500
Eliminate Tax Preferences for Oil and Gas Development	500

OTHER

Restore Non-Resident Withholding Tax to Treaty Rates	411
Introduce Minimum Tax on Profitable Corporations	400
Extend GST to Brokerage and Other Financial Services	190
Restore Tobacco Taxation to pre-1995 Level	495

ONE TIME TAXES

Surtax on Private Financial Institutions	1500
Enhanced Enforcement of Tax Regulations	600

8. Where We've Come From and Where We're Going: Paul Martin vs. the AFB

Now we're ready to compare the AFB with Paul Martin's budget, so that we can see clearly what the AFB is the alternative to. We have put the 1998-99 AFB and the 1997-98 Martin budget side by side. (When we put together the AFB each year, we always begin with the previous year's federal government budget.)

The purpose of this exercise is to encourage participants to think critically about neo-liberal values and AFB values. What do these budgets say about where we want to go as a country?

We have also added a number of other economic statistics: the gross domestic product (GDP), the unemployment rate, the real interest rate (adjusted for inflation), and the inflation rate. We've also added one extremely useful tool. We have taken the main areas of the budget and expressed them as a percentage of the GDP. The GDP is the total value of the goods and services produced in any given year in a country. It is a measuring stick that allows for clear comparisons between financial years. It also allows comparisons between countries. The European Union has set a standard that a country's debt is acceptable if it is 60 percent of GDP. (For a longer-term view of how the AFB manages the debt, refer to the AFB's five year plan in chapter 7.)

This is not to suggest that we believe the GDP to be the best tool for measuring the performance of an economy. We mention above in chapter 3 that many people, including some who work on the AFB, believe it to be a very flawed tool. We use it because it offers a useful comparison.

Exercise 7: Paul Martin vs. the AFB

Looking at the chart showing the two federal budgets, where can you see evidence of:

- Job creation strategies?
- The attitudes toward debt / deficit held by the budget makers?
- Support for social programs?

What can you say by looking at:

- Differences in the expenditure side?
- Differences in the economic indicators at the bottom of the page (such as inflation rate, unemployment, interest rates, and so on)?

Think about the revenue side and what has been outlined in chapter 7. Compare revenue as a percentage of GDP. What does this tell you?

Comparison of Martin Budget and AFB

	MARTIN 1997-98	AFB 1998-99
Program Spending		
National Social Investment Funds		
Health Care Fund	6.7	9.4
Post-Secondary Education Fund	2.3	3.1
Income Support Fund	5.5	7.5
Child Care Investment Fund	0.3	0.9
Housing Investment Fund	1.9	2.3
Retirement Fund	22.3	23.5
Unemployment Insurance Fund	13.2	14.2
Sub-Total NSIFs	52.2	60.9
Departmental Spending / Other:	53.6	57.8
Total Program Spending	105.8	118.7
Total Revenue	148.2	160.2
Operating Balance	42.4	41.5
Public Debt Charges	43.8	41.5
Total Expenditures	149.6	160.2
Surplus / (Deficit)	(1.4)	0.0
Net Public Debt	585.0	585.0
AS A PERCENTAGE OF GDP		
Revenues	17.5	17.8
Program Spending	12.5	13.2
Debt Charges	5.2	4.6
Deficit	0.1	0.0
Net Public Debt	68.9	65.0
ECONOMIC INDICATORS		
GDP	849.0	900.0
Real Interest Rate	2.4%	1.5%
Unemployment Rate	8.9%	7.9%
Inflation Rate	1.5%	2.0%

9. Process and Politics

The Alternative Federal Budget is the outgrowth of work that was started by the Winnipeg-based social justice coalition Cho!ces. Cho!ces was formed in 1990 following the election of a majority Conservative government in Manitoba. As the name suggests it sought to emphasize that there were alternatives to the policies that Gary Filmon's government was following. It sought to counter what has been referred to as the TINA syndrome, the assertion that there is no alternative to neo-conservative policies. From the outset Cho!ces combined social action with more traditional forms of research.

This final chapter should take the entire last afternoon if you're doing the full workshop. It includes an exercise, but your group may prefer instead to do concrete planning and organizing.

One of its core activities from 1991 onwards was the creation of an alternative provincial budget. This document would be released a few days prior to the delivery of the government budget. From there Cho!ces went on to produce alternative budgets for the Winnipeg School Board and the City of Winnipeg. These budgets have always been produced with the participation and support of community groups that have been affected by budget cuts.

Alternative budgets are meant to operate on a number of levels. They can, for example, be highly practical. Proposals in alternative budgets have been adopted by local governments. But they also serve to widen the range of political debate, to provide community activists with ammunition, and to stimulate debate and discussion within the left on economic and social issues. That's why, for example, we release our alternative budgets just before the release of the official ones. It gives us the maximum coverage in the press and brings the issues to the fore just when the government, or school board, or other official body, is putting out its own budget.

In 1994 Cho!ces sponsored a conference on alternative budgets. Out of that conference came the decision to explore the possibility of creating an Alternative Federal Budget. The pieces began to come together when the Canadian Labour Congress and the Canadian Centre for Policy Alternatives indicated their willingness to support the project. The result has been that since 1995 an annual Alternative Federal Budget has appeared as a joint project of Cho!ces and the Canadian Centre for Policy Alternatives.

In Manitoba, Cho!ces has continued with civic and provincial budgets. Provincial alternative budgets have been produced in Prince Edward Island, New Brunswick, Ontario, and Saskatchewan. There are now lots of people across the country, union members, activists of all stripes, academics, and other experts, who along with just plain folks have become involved in challenging the right-wing takeover of the social agenda in Canada. Doing alternative budgets has become part of the struggle for social justice.

The Politics of Alternative Budgets

The purpose behind our alternative budgets has always been politics, not economics. As we have suggested throughout this book, budgets are first and foremost about people, community, and politics—economics, computer programs and accounting come second and they are tools and servants, not masters. Economics, statistics, accounting, and computer programs are used to support and implement the choices made by people about how we should be able to live our lives together.

Paul Martin and Jean Chrétien, and before them, Michael Wilson and Brian Mulroney, and all those who have occupied the roles they play, would have us believe that making budgets is too complicated for ordinary people. That economics requires them to take a back seat to experts. They would have us believe that there is no alternative to cutbacks, higher unemployment and the slashing of social programs. They want us to believe that budget-making is some sort of higher science, understood and practised only by a small number of specially trained people. And they keep their budget making secret so that they can perpetuate this powerful myth. The purpose behind alternative budgets is to show that they lie.

We want to demystify budget-making and to help anyone who is interested get confident enough to criticize official budgets. Indeed, to criticize our own alternative budgets too. We want to show that you do not have to be an economist or an accountant to oversee budget-making—even a $150 billion budget. We want to show that if you can cope with your own budget at home, you can also deal fairly and sensibly with a $600 billion debt.

Chrétien, when he was Pierre Trudeau's finance minister, was not an economist. He was a small town lawyer. Paul Martin is not an accountant. He is a lawyer who ran a Canadian shipping company which has all its ships registered offshore rather than in Canada. Check out your own province. Most ministers in charge of the economy have not been economists or experts. Like most of the rest of us, they could not do the fancy numbers juggling and computer modelling required for contemporary budgets. But they can, and do, make the important decisions in budget-making.

Well so can you. Whether you are postal worker in St. John's, or a teacher in Deep Cove, whether you are a federal civil servant working in New Brunswick, or a student in Montréal, an autoworker in London, an anti-poverty activist in Saskatchewan, a massage therapist in Edmonton, an artist in Yellowknife, or a fisher in British Columbia, you can join in too. And together we can do a budget for Canada. We have. The AFB has had input from all these places and more.

And we can also do budgets for our school boards, our local councils, our transit company or a provincial government. We can get involved just like Chrétien did and Martin does now. With a process like the Alternative Federal Budget, we can all do it and we can do it together. Not a technocratic budget that works for only a few, but a realistic budget that is fair and balanced and is the result of political struggle between all those who participate. A budget based on a consensus among all of us who share the desire for a fairer government even though we differ greatly in our local concerns.

A major difference between our budget and Martin's is that we do it together and in the open. Martin, and before him Wilson and all those before him, do theirs in secret. With the AFB, and with alternative budgets generally, we want to show that anyone can do it. And do it well.

The Government Process

Our process is not much different from the process used by Martin or any other government budget-maker. His first step is to figure out the range of what is possible from an analysis of last year's numbers and the current political climate. He and his staff review the performance of the economy up to that point in the year and produce the *Economic and Fiscal Update*, which is usually made public in the fall. You see a slightly altered version of this update as Martin's budget alongside the AFB in chapter 8. (Incidentally, this is also the document that we use as the basis for the AFB.) They work out what the range of possibilities is, what taxes might be raised and how much, which ones lowered and how much, how much revenue to take in, how much might be spent. They figure out in a general way what they will be able to support for the coming year. This makes up their "fiscal framework."

Martin's mind isn't exactly open at this point. It's a very restricted view that he carries. He will not consider any approach to the deficit or debt other than that of the monetarists. He will follow the Friedmanite ideas that inflation is the issue and unemployment a solution. Excessively high profits and obscenely high salaries for the few he accepts with a shrug. For him, there is no alternative, and no need for one.

Then they consult. Martin holds his public consultations across the country. If you have ever been to one, you know they are dull affairs. More important than these public consultations to Martin are the private consultations he holds with the powerful people whose interests he will pursue in his budget. We are rarely told about these meetings and they are not public. Big corporations, the banks, no doubt his old friends from his days in big business and the legal profession, all have their input. Huge amounts of money, no one can be sure how much, are spent on lobbyists to get to him and influence him to place their interests uppermost in his budget. (To his credit, he even consults with the AFB! His verdict? "This is good. This is very good," he declared at one of his chats with folks from the AFB.)

Following our consultations, we put together and publish a framework document that outlines the policies that will influence the AFB. Martin does no such thing. His deliberations and decisions are done in secret and remain secret. The public never knows what policy decisions will guide his budget process.

Paul Martin is not too concerned about health care—he can afford the best treatment available out of his own pocket. He's not too concerned about unemployment. He's assured of positions on the boards of directors of big business for the rest of his life. He will almost certainly have all sorts of job offers when he leaves politics. And he's rich anyway. He's not too concerned about the crisis in the fisheries, its just another industry to invest in to him. Its not a job or a way of life. He's not too concerned about the plight of refugees or immigrants, the oppression of women, or child poverty. They are all too remote from him. He listens to his friends, to people like him, and he works out a budget that he feels comfortable with, and one that fits with his very restricted fiscal plan.

Then he gets the numbers people involved—the economists, computer modelling experts, and the accountant types. They check it out, the computer models making projections on the impact of the proposed budget for the upcoming years. If anything shows up in these projections that they don't want, such as too much inflation, Martin will adjust the budget. Once the numbers look good, they write it up, and with a long speech in Parliament, much ballyhoo, and a chorus of "There is no alternative," they release their new budget.

A few months later, they begin the process over for the next year's budget. Once more in secret. We do something similar, with some very particular, very democratic, differences.

The Politics of Our Process

Superficially, our process looks much the same. We work out generally what we think is possible. We consult. We publish a framework document setting out our ideas. And finally we turn to the numbers experts and produce our budget. But beyond this similar skeletal structure, we approach our task differently and with very different motives.

Unlike Chrétien / Martin, we don't do our budget-making secretly in Ottawa among a tight set of cronies. The AFB is a country-wide process conducted with an extremely diverse mass of people, organizations and institutions. Unions, NGOs, activist organizations, activists, union members, unemployed as well as employees engaged in all sorts of work, come together to produce the AFB. In fact, the participation is so diverse that it is almost surprising, sometimes, that we are able to produce a budget at all. It is exciting proof of the value of political *action* (as opposed to theory or wheeling and dealing) that a group so large and diverse can produce a coherent, workable document.

The Canadian Centre for Policy Alternatives is a think-tank with a broad membership. They are focused on the big picture, national trends and national responses. The CCPA works closely with the AFB's Ottawa Steering Committee which includes representation from the national union leadership and from national activist organizations.

Cho!ces' members are mostly activists. Individually they may be union local members, academics, workers in various positions, unionized or nonunion, unemployed, or still in the education system. Cho!ces works closely with the AFB's Winnipeg Working Group which also includes some other people who are active both locally and across the country. Cho!ces is represented on the Ottawa Steering Committee and the AFB exercise is coordinated by representatives of Cho!ces and the CCPA.

The funding for the AFB comes mostly from the unions. Volunteer participation is massive and essential for a credible, broad-based, politically effective budget making process. If one were to add to the funding provided by the union movement the value of the voluntary work and the considerable amounts contributed by union locals and activist organizations, the Alternative Federal Budget is probably a million dollar effort.

Beyond Ottawa and Winnipeg, the AFB gathers input from individuals and organizations across the country. And unlike Martin, we don't just consult: we involve all comers in the budget process. That's because we want anyone to be able to analyze and criticize, not only Martin's budget, but also the AFB itself and any other budgetary process that affects them.

It is for these political reasons that budget schools are offered across the country to share the knowledge and skills that have been developed through the years. *Show Us the Money* has evolved out of those budget schools. Union locals, coalitions of activists, social justice networks, ordinary Canadians, get together to support the budget schools, to contribute to the AFB and to hold budget launch meetings. With each budget, with each budget school, more people gain more confidence in their abilities to question the Martin budget and to say, loudly and clearly, that there are alternatives.

And that is the point. The AFB is not in itself a radical document. It represents a consensus built across the country as to what is possible today, in today's economic climate with today's debts and today's political realities. It is socially oriented, and it is *possible*. Above all it is a political exercise intended to build strength and solidarity across the country. It is a political exercise that shows that a broad democratic coalition of socially active persons and organizations can work, and work better than the secretive machinations of big business and big government.

THE STRUCTURE OF THE AFB

The creation of the Alternative Federal Budget is a six month process that usually starts in August. There are—roughly, since it is a fluid process—four main sets of players in the Alternative Federal Budget, although there is considerable overlap between these groups. As the process continues it is also our desire to include more people in the operation. Here are the four groups.

1. The Ottawa Steering Committee

This committee of close to 40 people brings together representatives from a wide range of organizations that seek to have input into the AFB. They include organized labour, church groups, women's organizations, environmental activists, anti-poverty organizations, anti-racism organizations, and the international development community. The committee meets on a monthly basis. The Steering Committee provides overall direction to the process. It reaches its decisions through consensus.

2. The Winnipeg Working Group

This is a group of 30 or so academics, policy experts and community activists, most of whom are affiliated with Cho!ces. They also meet monthly and work on a consensus basis. The Winnipeg Cho!ces office handles much of the day-to-day operations behind the creation of the budget.

The AFB has traditionally been co-coordinated by representatives from both the Ottawa Steering Committee and the Winnipeg Working Group. Material flows both ways between the two structures and the normal decision-making rule is double consensus. Final responsibility for the content of the budget lies with the Ottawa Steering Committee.

3. Policy Groups

The budget coordinators recruit people from across the country who will serve as policy chairs. It is these people's responsibility to assemble policy groups on the various budget areas. The policy groups generally meet by telephone. The chair of each policy group is responsible for writing the budget's policy statement on their policy area. All the policy papers are combined to form what is referred to as the framework document.

4. Public Input

This can take a variety of forms. Policy group chairs are encouraged to hold public consultations that allow people to comment on previous budgets and make recommendations for upcoming budgets. Budget schools are held across the country. At these schools the AFB proposals are presented and input into future budgets solicited.

These then are the four major players. There is no reason why in coming years other groups could not be added to the mix or the structure rebalanced.

The Process of the AFB

One of the first steps in the process of creating the budget is the establishment of a fiscal framework. This framework is based on an analysis of the broader trends in the economy. On the basis of this document, decisions can be made on the overall percentage that spending can be allowed to increase and the possibilities of increasing revenues. This framework is discussed, modified and accepted by the Ottawa Steering Committee, the Winnipeg Working Group, and the policy chairs.

At the same time, the policy groups prepare their draft policy papers. The deadline for these papers is usually the end of November. At this stage the policy papers are prepared without any statistics. Also at this time technical and background papers are prepared. These papers differ from the policy papers in that they are intended to stimulate ongoing discussion and are not necessarily reflected in the upcoming budget.

These documents are reviewed by the Winnipeg Working Group and the Ottawa Steering Committee and returned to the policy groups. The policy groups finalize their contributions for the Framework Document by mid-December.

The framework document is finalized by the steering committee and the working group. At this point the policy groups prepare text for the budget and attach figures to spending and revenue issues. The budget is finalized in late January and early February, during which time both the steering committee and the working group meet on a regular basis to make the trade-offs to build consensus for the final document.

Exercise 8: Making Choices

This exercise is devised to give the group a flavour of the Alternative Federal Budget process.

In the process of arriving at a new federal budget, participating groups and individuals have strong beliefs about what the federal government ought to be doing to help improve the lives of their constituencies. All of these interests and opinions must be heard, but in the end, a compromise position on what can and should be done in this year's alternative budget must be reached.

 Divide the participants into up to five small groups. Each of these small groups is to play the role of a policy group in preparing the AFB. As much as possible let the subjects choose which group they join. The groups

Say that the following five policy areas have representatives in the alternative budget process:

- Child Care
- Health
- Income Support
- Post-secondary Education
- Employment Insurance

The group responsible for each area has three pieces of knowledge from which to build a future direction that will work for all of the groups. They know the amount—in billions of dollars—that the Chrétien government spent on their area in 1996-97, the amount the government spent on the area in 1997-98, and the fact that the Alternative Federal Budget is capable of allowing for an overall spending increase of $9 billion on social programs.

Each group should discuss how they would like to see the delivery of programs in their area changed. Determine how much of an increase, in billions of dollars, they would like to see made in an alternative budget for each of the five policy areas.

What are the implications of choosing to live within spending restraints? To what degree can new ideas or policies develop when there is very little fiscal flexibility?

What would be the political implications for the AFB of choosing not to live within those spending constraints? Would it simply dissolve into a wish list? Would it be taken seriously? Should it?

should then present their proposals to the group as a whole. They should have a short one paragraph policy statement and a funding figure. It will be up to the group as a whole to allocate the nine billion dollars among these budget categories. For the sake of simplicity, the smallest figure that can be allocated should be a half a billion dollars. The decision must be reached by way of consensus and discussion.

What were the problems that people experienced with this exercise?

Among the ideas you may wish to introduce into the discussion are the problems that arise from lack of knowledge of how the system works, what the implications of changes are, and so forth. Point out that the AFB suffers from these problems in a number of ways. First of all, while there are numerous people who work on the budget who are experts in their field, there are gaps in their knowledge. More importantly, the types of experts we rely on are predominantly academics. As a consequence, when we deal with job creation, or income support, it is unlikely the policies are going to come from people whose expertise derives from being unemployed, or a single parent, or on social assistance.

SOCIAL PROGRAM SPENDING		
	1996-97	1997-98
HEALTH	7.4	6.7
INCOME SUPPORT	5.7	5.6
CHILD CARE	0.35	0.35
EMPLOYMENT INSURANCE	13.5	13.2
POST-SECONDARY EDUCATION	2.3	2.3

PUTTING THE NUMBERS TOGETHER

Economists' Endorsements

It is all too likely that professional economists are afforded too much credibility in commenting on matters of economic and budgetary policy in our political culture—the economy is far too important to be left up to them! But it is a fact of political life that if a set of policy measures can be shown to have the backing of numerous economists, then it is likely to carry more credibility in the eyes of the public who feel less competent in judging the relative merits of complicated economic policy. For this reason, the Alternative Federal Budget has attempted each year to obtain endorsements of the budget from a large number of economists.

Our definition of what constitutes an economist is rather broad (as it should be), and includes academics and researchers working in a range of other disciplines (such as political science, social work, and industrial relations). To obtain these endorsements, the planning committee first drafts a short letter summarizing the key features of ingredients in the alternative budget, and then asking respondents to endorse the major fiscal and economic thrust of the budget. The letter is circulated to poten-

As policies, rough program spending, and revenue figures are being developed, the experts get involved doing the more technical work on the economics of the budget. As with the Martin budget, their role is a vital one, making sure, as much as possible, that what we are proposing will do what we want and expect. They don't take over. They perform a set of functions that are essential and without which we couldn't produce a sound practical budget.

Their job is the technical one of fiddling with the numbers, running them through a computer program that will show how our budget numbers are likely to work through the next few years. That will show what won't work and what will. And just as with Martin's process, our experts can listen and suggest alternatives. They are an integral part of our politics.

Like Martin, we do not need to know exactly how the numbers folks do their work. That said, it is still useful to have some idea of what they do. If we are really going to demystify the budgetary process and really build for ourselves the confidence to argue with the Martins of the world, it is useful to have an understanding of what experts do and how it helps.

The Fiscal Planning Spreadsheet

A central tool in the alternative budgeting process is a simple accounting framework with which the budget-makers can develop a sense of how much they will be able to spend, and how the funds will be raised. This accounting tool is called a fiscal planning spreadsheet. The most effective way to construct this simple fiscal spreadsheet is with a computer software package such as Lotus 1-2-3 or Quattro Pro. Across the top of this spreadsheet are listed the relevant budget years. These should include the current fiscal year, one or two years of historical data (for comparison purposes), the years for which the alternative budget will be developed (usually two future years), and then any additional future years for which longer term forecasts may be relevant. Down the left side of the spreadsheet, list the major economic and fiscal categories needed to develop the fiscal plan. These will usually include: GDP, growth rate of GDP (broken down between real growth and inflation, if desired), interest rate (both a common broad interest rate, such as 90-day, and the actual average rate paid by the government on its debt), total government revenues, total program spending (all spending other than interest payments), interest payments, the budget balance (surplus or deficit), accumulated government debt.

If the alternative budget is making predictions or policies affecting employment levels, the planning spreadsheets may also include some labour market data (such as employment, labour force participation, and the unemployment rate). Data for all of these items can be filled in for the current and previous years. Then the spreadsheet can be extended forward in time, step by step. Since general economic conditions are crucial to the state of public finances, we need to start with some forecast of economic growth, inflation, and interest rates. Many forecasts are prepared for Canada as a whole by economists, banks, and other institutions. At the provincial level, forecasts are developed by the Conference Board of Canada which are usually publicly available in a university library (and are usually summarized in newspaper reports), and by the major banks. Alternative budget-makers can choose a particular forecast, or an average of several forecasts, or they can even specify their own forecast (if for some reason they do not believe the conventional forecasts). For a civic budget, forecasts of local economic growth may be available; if not, it is usually safe to use forecast growth rates for the provincial economy.

The selected forecast should be adjusted to reflect the likely impact of the alternative budget itself on the national or regional economy. For example, if the alternative budget includes major new spending or job-creation initiatives, then this may increase the rate of economic growth above what would be expected in the conventional forecasts. A credible estimate can be made of this effect, and then added to the conventional growth forecast. For example, if the alternative budget plans to increase public works spending by $1 billion, then the expected level of nominal GDP would equal the current year GDP, times the expected growth rate (both inflation and real growth), plus the additional public works spending. This adjustment to GDP can even be increased by some multiplier factor such as 1.25 or 1.50 reflecting the fact that government spending can lead to even larger ultimate increases in GDP as the new spending is cycled and recycled through the national or regional economy. Similarly, major changes in tax policy will also affect the rate of future economic growth. A major increase in taxes will slow growth, while a cut in taxes will increase growth. The precise amount of growth added or subtracted will depend on the type of tax being adjusted. In general, if taxes are being raised by $1 billion, then future GDP should be reduced by about three-quarters of that amount ($750 million), and similarly, lowering taxes would require us to increase the future GDP.

How does the expected rate of economic growth affect the budget planning process? Base tax revenues generally rise in step with economic activity. A safe first approximation can be made by assuming that basic total tax revenues will grow at the same rate as

tial endorsers, and hopefully followed up with personal appeals. Sympathetic local economists can assist in generating lists of potential endorsers, and in distributing the appeal.

nominal GDP (that is, the sum of real GDP growth plus consumer price inflation). Another way of doing this is to multiply total expected GDP by the current year tax ratio (taxes as a share of GDP). Adjustments can then be made to this estimate according to any major tax policy changes planned as part of the alternative budget itself. For example, if the alternative budget plans a new $1 billion tax on high-income households, then the government's revenues would be expected to grow by the same percentage as the growth of nominal GDP, plus the additional $1 billion.

A forecast of the government's debt service charges can also be generated, as follows. Calculate a running total of accumulated debt, equal to the previous year's debt plus any current year deficit (or minus any current year surplus). Then multiply this forecast debt burden by the average rate of interest that the government is expected to be paying. This average rate of interest will reflect a number of factors, including current and expected broader interest rates, and the rate at which existing debt is turned over into new bonds and loans. As a starting assumption, use the same average interest rate that was paid last year (equal to the government's debt service charges divided by the last year's accumulated debt), and then adjust that rate up or down for future years depending on expected trends in interest rates. In the case of the Alternative Federal Budget, the forecast of interest rates is also adjusted to incorporate the effects of the budget itself for example, by assuming lower broader interest rates (thanks to changes in the policy stance of the Bank of Canada), or by assuming the refinancing of a share of existing debt through the Bank of Canada. Keep in mind that these policy levers are not available to lower levels of government.

Once forecasts have been generated of total revenue and debt service charges, two key variables in the budget remain to be determined: program spending and the final budget balance (deficit or surplus). Two rough approaches can be adopted to this final planning phase, depending on the policy priorities of the alternative budget-makers. The budget-makers may wish to set themselves some type of a budget target for example, to keep the budget balanced, or to generate a $1 billion surplus, or to ensure that the deficit is no larger than one percent of GDP. In this case, the budget balance is set as a matter of policy. The amount of funds available for program spending then falls out, as a residual. In other words, the planning spreadsheet tells the budget-makers how much they can spend on programs, consistent with their economic assumptions, their tax measures, and their budgetary target.

An alternative approach is to simply specify how much program spending the budget makers want to include in their budget. In this case, the final budget balance is then determined as a residual. In this case, the planning spreadsheet tells the budget-makers how large of a deficit or surplus they are likely to incur, in light of their economic assumptions, tax measures, and program spending desires. If the resulting deficit is too large, the planners can go back and consider additional taxes to impose, or reduce the level of program spending. Indeed, the whole fiscal planning process is likely to be an iterative one. Initial planning spreadsheets can be presented to the alternative budget committee, to provide budget-makers with an initial idea of the range of choices and constraints they are facing. Subsequent fine-tuning of the spreadsheet will reflect changing views on taxes, spending, deficit-reduction, and interest rate policies. The spreadsheet will be adjusted several times until a final version is developed consistent with the wishes of the budget committee. Given the interconnected nature of the budget arithmetic, and the fact that the planning spreadsheet is likely to be revised often, you can see that it is a good idea to build the spreadsheet on a computer.

The final budget must also include a breakdown of program spending between its different specific departments and projects (although this detailed breakdown is not necessary for the initial planning discussions). A good way to generate this breakdown is as follows. Start with the departmental breakdown from the current year's budget. Then increase the projected spending for each department area based on whatever particular projects are being proposed in that area. Budget-makers will probably have to trade-off these new projects against reductions in funding for some other departments considered less important. This assignment of future budgets will continue in an iterative fashion until the bottom-line total program spending matches the total program spending allowed for in the fiscal planning spreadsheet. It may help to have a large catch-all (or residual) category, comprised of several less important departments or administrative funds, in order to help attain this final balancing.

Economic Simulations

As a tool for fine-tuning the fiscal planning process, and also to help improve the credibility of the budget in public-relations and lobbying, it may be useful to conduct an economic simulation of the effects of the alternative budget. At the level of the Alternative Federal Budget, these simulations have been conducted by the consulting firm Informetrica. An economic simulation is conducted in the following manner. An economic researcher constructs a computerized model of the national or regional economy. This model takes as input certain assumptions about government policy measures (including spending, taxes, interest rates, and other issues). The model produces forecasts of economic variables such as employment, GDP growth, and inflation. The goal of the simulation is to estimate the ultimate impact of the alternative budget on those key output variables. So the economist adjusts the modelling assumptions to reflect the policy measures contained in the alternative budget. Then they re-run the computer model to estimate the levels and changes in GDP, employment, and inflation in light of the effects of the alternative budget. The total impact of the budget can then be estimated

Budget workshops like these are very important. Probably the main obstacle to people's participation in an alternative budget process is the intimidation involved in working with numbers and economics. This workshop is meant to show that putting together a budget can be done in a democratic fashion, by ordinary people. By demystifying the budget process, we become more comfortable in both challenging how the government does its budgeting, and in proposing our own alternatives.

In 1998, workshops to help activists make use of alternative budgets were held in over twenty communities from St. John's to Victoria. With the help of this material, many more workshops should be possible.

As a final exercise, the participants should gather into small groups one more time. Each group should discuss the following three questions and come up with brief comments and concrete suggestions.

by comparing these new forecasts to the original (or "base case") forecast that the economist generated on the basis of conventional budget assumptions. It is very difficult to start from scratch with this type of simulation, since the work involved in building up the initial computer model of the economy is quite substantial. It is better to approach some economists who have access to an existing model, and ask them to perform the simulation of the impact of the alternative budget. This may be difficult in regions for which economic models do not exist, or are only available at high cost from private consultants. Sympathetic economists from a local university may be able to offer advice on how these simulations could be arranged.

PROMOTIONAL STRATEGY

The AFB is released to the public in February. Each year the intent is to have more community groups participate in the release and its popularization. In fact, there have been greater numbers of communities involved in the launching of the AFB each year.

In 1998, public events to release the AFB were held in over thirty communities across Canada. It is very rare that the media totally ignore these events. The AFB now has a national public profile, which has been useful in getting attention for other alternative budgets, such as those at the provincial or civic level. The credibility of alternative budgets as a political tool is now recognized by most media and by the public, and is growing.

As any activist can tell you, there are no guarantees when it comes to media attention, but we have put together some basic ideas and suggestions for how to interest the media in an alternative budget.

LOCAL MEDIA

Popular Materials

Not everyone will have the time or interest to read an entire alternative budget. Prepare easy to read versions of the budget to communicate its basic points. Brochures can be mailed out on their own or as part of other mailings. A tabloid is one important part of our strategy to publicize the AFB.

What's the Media After?

- Something new
- An interesting angle / hook to the news
- Human interest—something they can show affects people's lives directly
- Conflict
- Something associated with the credible, the powerful, or media stars
- Something that other media have picked up on

General Hints and Strategies for Media Work

Analyze the kind of news coverage your outlets do and tailor your approach. Soften up the media. Invest some time talking to media types: providing background for them, explaining the importance of what you are doing, finding them a news hook that they are likely to use.

Be opportunistic. When some event or issue comes along where your alternative budget is relevant, use it. A national campaign like the AFB can often be attached to local issues of relevance.

Release your alternative budget before the official version. Begin planning for the release well in advance. The first step is to make media aware of the AFB and your group. Send out a media release introducing yourself and the AFB, and perhaps some background material. Send it to assignment editors, news directors, specific beat reporters and any reporters you know to be sympathetic.

Follow up with calls to selected newsrooms, individuals who you consider most important for coverage. Reiterate the importance of the AFB and if they claim ignorance, repeat basic information and offer to the send material again, because they may very well have thrown the first lot in the garbage.

About a week before the event, send out a media release announcing the upcoming AFB launch media conference. The day before the launch send a reminder media release and follow with phone calls to key media outlets asking if they are going to attend your media conference and how you can accommodate them later if they can't make it.

Don't make the job of media types difficult. Pay attention to their deadlines. Be polite and constructive even when you have to be firm about following your agenda. Make media conference times and locations media friendly. Write clear media releases that give the media an angle on the story. A media release is not a pamphlet; usually it is designed simply to give basic information and capture media attention. Keep presentations short and ask for questions.

Try to find an appropriate location for your media conference—it can reinforce your message. Be sure to invite everyone who has participated in any way in the budget process to the media conference.

1. How can alternative budgets—federal, provincial, or municipal—play a useful role in your community?

2. How do you think the structure we currently use for the AFB could be broadened to include more people's input? Think about how the AFB structure and process could include more members of your community, and write a proposal giving recommendations for change and growth.

3. What could be done in your community to increase the impact of the AFB? Design a plan to make this happen.

Clearly identify media spokespeople who are capable of speaking in soundbites. You should have a spokesperson the media can call even after your event or media release is cold. They may decide to use you or your material in connection with something else later. For example, the next time a reporter is looking for an opinion from the left they might think of you.

After the launch, issue a media release. If you're launching an Alternative Federal Budget, talk about other releases across Canada, especially quoting positive reaction from media in other centres. Remind the media that you are available to comment on the official government budget when it is released.

If you get no coverage phone the news directors and ask why not. If you get bad coverage call news directors and tell them how it was bad. If you get fair and balanced coverage, thank the news director and specific reporters if you have developed a relationship which allows that.

Complement them on their professionalism. Don't get sweet and sucky. Sympathetic reporters must still act in a professional manner. Some editorialists have a mandate to write from a specific perspective. If it is from a sympathetic perspective do not take them for granted. Take good care of them and thank them, too.

For specific advice or feedback on your media strategy and plans, consult local communications types from groups you trust, such as labour or social service organizations.

Glossary

adjusted for inflation: In a market economy, many economic items are expressed in monetary units. With inflation, the value of these monetary units will change. For example, high inflation makes a given amount of money worth less, since it cannot buy as many goods or services as it could before the inflation. When the value of money changes, it makes it more difficult to measure the value of other items. By adjusting for inflation, the value of money is stable, and then it can be used as a fixed standard unit of measurement. Economic statistics that are adjusted for inflation are referred to as real magnitudes, such as real interest rates, real wages and real GDP.

assets: This is what the government owns or what is owed to it. Unlike private corporations, the federal government does not show assets on its balance sheet, which can provide a misleading picture. Many government assets—national parks for example—are extremely difficult to put a value on.

Bank of Canada: A federal agency which controls interest rates and the money supply. It influences interest rates by setting rates on short-term loans that it makes to chartered banks. The Bank of Canada can also purchase government bonds or allow the private sector to purchase bonds.

bonds: A bond is essentially a loan. The government sells interest-bearing bonds to finance the deficit. Increasingly these bonds have been purchased by non-Canadians, which gives them greater control over government policy.

budget: A statement delivered by the finance minister outlining the government's spending and taxation plans for the coming year. Budgets are significant because they represent a statement of the government's values and because the government's spending and taxation plans have an impact on the broader economy. The key elements in a budget are revenue, expenditures, debt / assets, deficit / surplus, and debt servicing charges.

> **revenue:** The various incomes and payments received by the government. The most important source of revenues are taxes.

> **expenditures:** The different expenditures and payments made by the government. These include expenditures for government programs, transfers to other levels of government, to corporations and to private individuals, and debt servicing charges.

> **debt / assets:** Governments can and do borrow money. When they do, they incur a debt. The government debt expresses the amount of money the government owes to private individuals,

corporations and other governments. This debt is a liability to the government, but it is also an asset for those to whom the government owes the money. The government itself also has assets. These include public lands, public buildings, and financial assets such as foreign currency and gold.

deficit / surplus: If, in a given time period, such as a year, revenues are equal to expenditures, then the budget is balanced. If revenues are less than expenditures, the government budget has a deficit. If revenues exceed expenditures, the government budget has a surplus.

debt servicing charges: When governments borrow, they usually must pay interest on their loans. The debt servicing charges are the interest payments that the government makes on those loans that comprise the government debt.

Canada Health and Social Transfer: This new transfer payment to the provincial governments provides them with funding for health, post-secondary education, and social assistance. Previously, there had been separate funding arrangements for health, post-secondary education, and social assistance. Also there had been a commitment from the federal government to match provincial spending on a number of key areas. Both have been eliminated since the introduction of the CHST.

capital: This usually refers to assets such as factories, offices, machinery, and tools. These are the goods that are needed in production and generally last many years.

capital flight: A situation which occurs when financial investors act to transfer some or possibly all of their financial wealth, including stocks, bonds and currency, out of a particular country. The transfer usually is achieved by investors selling their financial assets in exchange for foreign currency. The result can be a dramatic fall in stock and bond prices, as well as a drop in the exchange rate. This situation may occur when the financial community is apprehensive about the security and profitability of their investments and businesses in a particular country.

capital gains: This is the profit that is made by selling a capital asset. Capital gains are taxed at a lower rate than income earned through wages and salaries.

chartered banks: Privately owned financial institutions that are allowed to operate as banks in Canada under a charter specified in the Bank Act. Canadian banking is dominated, at present, by the "big five" chartered banks: The Royal Bank, The Bank of Montreal, The Canadian Imperial Bank of Commerce, The Toronto Dominion Bank, and The Bank of Nova Scotia. In the last few years, these banks have announced record levels of profits.

classical economics: The school of thought first developed in the eighteenth century by Adam Smith. This theory held that there was no need for government regulation of the economy since the invisible hand of the market would lead to the best possible results.

corporate income tax: The money that the government collects from taxes on corporate profits.

Crown corporation: A corporation that is owned by the government, rather than by private individuals. These corporations have their own financial accounts, and are therefore not included as part of the government's budget.

debt servicing charges: If the government has a debt it must pay interest on the debt. The debt servicing charge is the amount of interest to be paid that year.

debt: If a government runs a deficit in one year, that deficit becomes part of the government debt the following year. The debt is funded by the Bank of Canada and by selling bonds. These bonds are bought by Canadians and by foreign investors.

deduction: A tax deduction simply means that a corporation or an individual is allowed to deduct this amount from their income, and therefore do not have to pay taxes on that amount. This is often referred to as writing something off on one's taxes.

defence: Federal funding for national defence.

deficit / surplus: If the government is spending more money in expenditures than it receives in revenue it is in a deficit position. The difference between revenue and expenditure is the deficit. If the government is taking in more in revenues than it is paying in expenditures it is in a surplus position. In this case the difference between revenue and expenditure is the surplus.

deficit financing: When expenditures exceed revenues, governments can cover this shortfall by borrowing money, such as by issuing bonds to private individuals or corporations. This form of deficit finance results in an increase in the government debt. In Canada, the federal government also has the option of printing additional money. This increases the money supply, and is known as monetization of the debt.

employment insurance (EI): Formerly called unemployment insurance, this program provides income support to unemployed Canadians. Where it once provided support to nearly 90 percent of the unemployed, its criteria have been tightened to the point where it now covers less than half of the unemployed.

    EI payments: The amount paid to Employment Insurance recipients.

    EI premiums: The money that employers and employees pay into the employment insurance fund.

expenditure: The amount of money the government expects to spend in the coming year on government programs.

fiscal policy: Government taxing and spending policies. (As opposed to monetary policy, which refers to government money supply and interest rate policies.) Fiscal policies are set out directly in the budget, while monetary policy is set out by the Bank of Canada.

Friedman, Milton: A conservative Nobel Prize winning economist from the University of Chicago. He is one of the founders and leading exponents of monetarism. His arguments for minimal government intervention in the economy are based upon a strong belief in the efficiency and desirability of a free, unregulated, market economy.

genuine progress indicator (GPI): An indicator designed to transcend the limitations of GDP as a measure of socio-economic progress and wellbeing. In calculating GPI, expenditures used to alleviate or remedy undesirable consequences of economic activity, such as environmental cleanup, are deducted from, instead of added to, the GPI totals. The GPI also attempts to impute value to various non-market activities, and then include these values as a component of the indicator.

Goods and Services Tax (GST): A tax that is paid by people when they purchase goods or services. It is sometimes called a consumption tax.

government operations: The funding of various government operations such as the departments of Agriculture, Justice, Heritage, Northern Affairs, Fisheries, Foreign Affairs, and so forth.

green economics: An economics which attempts to explicitly include the ecosystem and environmental factors in social decision making.

green taxes: Taxes imposed on various products or activities so that their costs will more accurately reflect their true environmental costs. By raising costs and thereby making these pursuits relatively more expensive, such taxes will act to encourage firms and individuals to engage in less environmentally destructive activities.

gross domestic product (GDP): The total value of the goods and services produced in Canada in any given year.

Hobsbawm, Eric: A British Marxist historian, best known for his three volume history of the "long" nineteenth century (*The Age of Revolution*, *The Age of Capital*, and *The Age of Empire*) and his recent history of the "short" twentieth century (*The Age of Extremes*).

inflation: A general increase in prices. It is usually described as a yearly percentage increase. Inflation is often attributed to a situation in which there is too much money chasing too few goods, thus driving up the price of all goods. Neo-classical economists blame inflation on low unemployment.

infrastructure: The networks of durable capital goods that comprise the physical structures that support other forms of economic and social activity. Examples include the transportation and communication networks (such as airports, canals, highways, pipelines, telephone lines), but also facilities such as sewage treatment plants. The importance of a sound and efficient infrastructure for other economic activities has been used as an argument for public support and even public provision of various types of infrastructure projects.

interest rates: An interest rate represents the cost of borrowing money. It is the percentage of the loan that must be paid back as well as the loan. Interest rates are often spoken of as being either nominal interest rates or real interest rates. A nominal interest rate is the actual rate that has to be paid. If you borrow $100 and have to pay back $105 at the end of the year, the nominal interest rate is 5 percent. However, the real interest rate is calculated by subtracting the rate of inflation from the interest rate. If in the example just given the rate of inflation for that year was 1 percent, the real interest rate would have been 4 percent, not 5 percent. High interest rates usually lead to high unemployment.

Keynes, John Maynard: An English economist who, in his 1936 book *The General Theory of Employment, Interest and Money*, argued that chronic unemployment could both exist and persist in a capitalist market economy. Keynes insisted that governments could and should intervene to alleviate economic depressions and to stabilize the economy.

Keynesianism: An economic theory which argues that the visible hand of the government must take action to increase demand during periods of high unemployment. According to this theory it is often necessary to engage in deficit spending to increase demand.

labour market: A market in which workers sell their labour time and employers purchase that time for a wage.

macroeconomic and microeconomic: A broadly-based classification of much of economic thought. Macroeconomics usually refers to economic issues that concern the performance of the economy on a national scale. Unemployment, inflation, trade, interest rates, and government budgets are prominent macroeconomic topics. Microeconomics has a narrower, more specific focus. It deals with the economic activity of a small number of agents, or of the examination of a particular type of market. The impact of specific types of taxes, the effects of new technologies in a particular industry, and the consequences of government regulation or deregulation, are some typical microeconomic topics.

Martin, Paul Jr.: Minister of Finance for the federal Liberal government for most of the 1990s.

Marx, Karl: A nineteenth century German economist and philosopher. He was the coauthor (with Frederick Engels) of the *Communist Manifesto*. His major economic work was the three volumes of *Capital*. For Marx, capitalism was a dynamic social and economic system. He argued that capitalism develops the productive powers of a society, which contributes to a great accumulation of wealth. However, this is a system based on exploitation, and one that is also destructive of people, of their communities, and of the natural world in which they live.

monetary policy: Government policies on money supply and interest rates (as opposed to fiscal policy which deals with taxing and spending). Monetary policy is set out by the Bank of Canada and is not formally included in the budget.

neo-classical economics (sometimes called neo-conservative or even neo-liberal): A theory which calls for deregulation of the economy in order to allow markets to set prices for all commodities, including labour.

nominal interest rate: This refers to an interest rate that has not been adjusted for inflation. The interest rates that are advertised by financial institutions, or that are quoted in the financial pages, are all nominal interest rates.

nominal prime interest rate: This is the interest rate that banks will charge for loans to their best customers.

old age security: The amount that the federal government spends on old age security and Guaranteed Income Supplements to Canadians over 65.

operating balance: Total revenues minus total program spending.

other revenue: A line in the federal budget which covers a wide range of miscellaneous issues.

other transfers: A general term covering miscellaneous government expenditures.

personal income tax: The money that the government collects from taxes on income.

postwar accord: After the Second World War, collective bargaining in Canada and the United States produced a large number of contracts in which workers ceded to management the right to introduce technological improvements into the workplace in return for wage increases explicitly tied to the productivity gains resulting from those improvements. This arrangement contributed to the period of rising real wages and the relatively high rates of economic growth that characterised the 1950s and 1960s. This accord broke down in the economic crises of the 1970s and 1980s.

poverty rate: The percentage of households whose income falls below the poverty line set by Statistics Canada.

program spending: The portion of total budgetary expenditures that goes to pay for various government programs and services. In the budget, program spending is equal to total expenditures minus debt servicing charges.

progressive tax: A tax system which places higher tax rates upon those who have a greater ability to pay.

real interest rate: The interest rate after an adjustment for inflation has been made. Real interest rates are considered to give a more accurate indication of the actual cost of borrowing or lending. Real interest rates can be calculated simply by subtracting the inflation rate from the nominal interest rate.

real prime interest rate: The difference between the nominal prime interest rate and the inflation rate.

regressive tax: A tax where the ratio of taxes paid relative to income decreases as income increases.

revenue: The amount of money the government expects to take in during the coming year. Over half of the Canadian government's revenue comes from personal income taxes.

short-term loans: Money that is borrowed and lent for relatively short time periods, usually a year or less. An important example of short term loans are the 90-day treasury bills of the federal government.

Smith, Adam: An eighteenth century Scottish economist best known for his book *The Wealth of Nations*. Smith coined the phrase "the invisible hand" in reference to his argument that, by leaving private individuals to pursue their own private interests, a competitive market economy will "invisibly" manipulate the economy to produce harmonious and desirable economic results for the society as a whole.

stabilizers: Elements of the macroeconomy which act to cushion the economy from the extremes of the booms and busts in the business cycle. In Canada, important stabilizers include the tax system and some social programs such as welfare and unemployment insurance.

stagflation: A situation in which the economy is simultaneously experiencing high inflation and low (or even negative) rates of economic growth.

think-tank: An institution, staffed by researchers and policy analysts, who research, publish and comment upon contemporary social and economic policy issues.

total expenditures: Total program spending plus debt servicing charges.

total program spending: The amount the government spends on all its programs in a single year.

transfers to crown corporations: Federal government funding of crown corporations such as the Canadian Broadcasting Corporation.

transfers to governments: The amount of money the federal government transfers to provincial governments. A very large portion of this money is meant to fund health care, post-secondary education, and welfare.

unemployment: An economic and social condition in which some workers would prefer to have jobs but do not actually have any at the moment. There are different types and states of unemployment. These include:

chronic unemployment: Unemployment which is long term and persistent.

frictional unemployment: The unemployment that results from the fact that, in a dynamic economy, there are at any given moment some workers who have just entered the labour force to look for work, or who have left their previous job but have not yet found or started a new one. Frictional unemployment is considered to be relatively short term and temporary for any individual worker.

full employment: A situation in which there may still be unemployment, but in which that unemployment would be entirely frictional. With full employment, the number of job seekers would not exceed the number of job vacancies.

structural unemployment: Unemployment which results from a mismatch between workers and jobs. This could result from a mismatch of skills (for example, vacancies for welders and unemployed teachers) or from a mismatch in location (for example, vacancies in Calgary, unemployed workers in Toronto).

unemployment rate: The percentage of Canada's labour force (those Canadians who are working or looking for work) that does not have work. The unemployment rate does not count people who have given up looking for work or those who are working part-time but would prefer to work full-time.

Waring, Marilyn: A feminist economist from New Zealand, best known for her groundbreaking work on the failure of standard GDP accounting to value domestic work, the burden of which falls disproportionately on women globally, and the consequent blindness of national policy towards women.

workfare: A social program in which individuals are required to perform labour in order to be deemed eligible for welfare payments. Workfare increases the pool of low wage labour, and by allowing public and private employers access to these workers, can act to contain and even undermine existing wages and working conditions.

A Note on the Handouts and Overheads

While this book is designed to be read by anyone who has an interest in the way budgets are put together and specifically in the politics and process of alternative budgets, we hope that many of you will find a way to go beyond simply reading the book and will become involved in an alternative budget project of your own.

To that end, we have put together the following set of overheads and handouts that can be used in an Alternative Federal Budget workshop. They are not meant to be "complete," and are simply a selection of materials that we feel may be particularly useful if you're leading a workshop. They are intended to be easy to photocopy.

Of course, ideally there would be a copy of this book available to every participant. If that's not possible, we'd suggest photocopying some combination of the preceding pages and the handouts and overheads that follow. As well, don't hesitate to come up with your own materials to emphasise what you think is important in a way with which you're comfortable.

Introduction to the
Alternative Budget Workshop

The objectives of this workshop are to provide participants with:

- Basic economic literacy
- A critique of the values that are now creating budgets
- An understanding of the Alternative Federal Budget
- A chance to come up with alternatives of their own

Others?

-
-
-
-
-

An introduction to the Alternative Federal Budget (AFB)

The idea of alternative budgeting arose as a response to politicians who claimed that they had no choice but to introduce neo-conservative policies. In the early 1990's, CHO!CES, a Winnipeg based coalition for social justice began to get people involved in preparing alternative budgets at the provincial, civic and school board levels. An Alternative Federal Budget has been prepared by activists across the country under the leadership of CHO!CES and the Canadian Centre for Policy Alternatives (Ottawa) since 1995. An important function of these alternative budgets is the participatory manner in which they are put together, drawing upon volunteers from all walks of life and especially those most affected by different aspects of the budgets in question. Opening up the budgeting process enables people to see how budgets are put together, how trade offs are made and to appreciate the real versus imagined budgetary constraints that governments have to work within. The AFB is not meant to be the only alternative, but its existence makes it clear that there are progressive alternatives.

Questions for Participants

- What organizations or community activities are you involved in?
- Why are you here and what do hope to learn?
- If there was one thing you could include in a federal budget, what would it be?

Budget Basics:
Introducing Alternative Budgets

The following is a list of economic terms that you may need to know during the course of this workshop, and their definitions. The glossary at the end of *Show Us the Money* also contains some commonly used economic terms.

Budget

A budget is a plan or an estimate for the spending and income for the coming year.

Revenue

The income that is expected in the coming year.

Expenditure

The amount of spending that is likely to take place in the coming year.

Surplus / Deficit

The difference between revenue and expenditure. If there is money left over, there is a surplus. If expenses exceed revenue, there is a deficit.

Debt / Assets

The total value of the organization. If there was a deficit this becomes part of the debt. Assets refer to those items of worth, which the organization owns and could sell.

Debt Servicing Charges

If there is debt, interest must be paid on the debt. Many lenders do not care if the debt is paid as long as you continue to make interest payments.

The Price is Right

The following exercise is designed to get you thinking about budgets. The table below shows the 1998-99 federal budget. We would like you to fill in the blanks for the following budget lines: personal income tax, corporate income tax, public debt charges, and deficit / surplus, net public debt. Some figures have been provided to help you get your bearings. The purpose of this exercise is not to get the "right" answers, but rather to familiarize you with budgets and the relationship between budget items.

The 1998-99 Federal Budget

(All figures in billions of dollars.)

REVENUE

Personal Income Tax
Corporate Income Tax
EI Premiums
GST
Excise taxes
Other revenue

TOTAL REVENUE   151.0

EXPENDITURE

Old age security
EI Payments
Transfers to governments
Other transfers
Transfers to Crown Corps
Defence
Government operations

TOTAL PROGRAM SPENDING   104.5

OPERATING BALANCE   46.5

PUBLIC DEBT CHARGES

TOTAL EXPENDITURES

SURPLUS / (DEFICIT)

NET PUBLIC DEBT

1. Personal Income Tax

The amount of money the government expects to receive from taxing individuals.

2. Corporate Income Tax

The amount of money the government expects to receive from taxing corporations.

3. Public Debt Charges

The amount of money the government expects to pay on the money it owes.

4. Deficit / Surplus

The expected difference between government revenues and government expenditures.

5. Net public debt

The total amount of money that the government owes. Deficits from previous years added together make up the total debt.

Price is Right: 1998 – 89 Figures

(All figures in billions of dollars.)

1. Personal Income Tax   71.0

2. Corporate Income Tax   20.5

3. Public Debt Charges   43.5

4. Deficit / Surplus   3.0

5. Net Public Debt   583.2

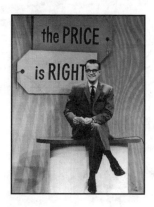

How We Got Here: A Layperson's History of Economics

Adam Smith

In his book *The Wealth of Nations*, published in 1776 just as the industrial revolution was getting underway, economist Adam Smith laid the groundwork for what is termed laissez-faire economics or classical economics. He believed that left to themselves competitive markets would create order, not disorder. If every member of society simply pursued his or her economic self-interest, all of society would benefit. Adam Smith's ideas ruled economic thinking in Canada up until the 1940s.

Karl Marx

Karl Marx lived in Europe in the middle of the nineteenth centruy. He believed that western societies were made up of classes, which act to defend and advance their interests. The two central classes in a modern economy, he argued, are the workers and the employers, who are in in conflict with one another. Marx encourages us to ask who is on top and who benefits from economic policy.

John Maynard Keynes

John Maynard Keynes was a British economist in the middle twentieth century. Keynes argued that sometimes the invisible hand of government needs to intervene in the economy. Keynes' ideas formed the basis of government economic policy from the 1940s to the 1970s. Keynesianism is associated with the practice of governments running deficits in lean times to balance the economy.

Milton Friedman

Milton Friedman is a neo-classical economist who favoured a return to laissez-faire economics. Neo-classical economists reject government deficit spending and believe that high rates of unemployment are needed to control wages and inflation. They believe that once the deficit is eliminated and social programs are reduced, wages and prices should decline and the economy will grow. His ideas have come to dominate government thinking since the early 1980s.

Responses to Neo-classical Economics

The new Friedmanite economic orthodoxy of the market is being challenged from the left. Quesitons are being raised about what we count and what we assign value to in the economy by economists influenced by feminism, environmentalism, and community economic development.

Ideas in Action: A Short Economic History Of the Twentieth Century

Eric Hobsbawm

The British historian Eric Hobsbawm has divided the history of our century into three ages. It should be noted that this history captures the Canadian, not the global experience. And within the Canadian experience are many groups and individuals whose experiences run counter to the general experience. (Aboriginal people for instance)

The Age of Catastrophe: 1900 – 1945

From 1900 to 1945 we experienced two world wars and two worldwide depressions. Economic competition drove nations to war, while a belief that governments should not interfere in the economy prolonged the depressions. During these years: there was no national health care program, welfare was funded by municipalities, schools were forced to close, there was no unemployment insurance, and workers could be fired for joining unions. The ideas of Adam Smith and the classical economists dominated this age. It was believed that governments should not and could not create jobs. Politicians, while expressing their sympathy for the poor and unemployed, felt government support would only rob them of their work ethic.

The Golden Age: 1945 – 1975

The ideas of the classical economists were discredited by the Second World War. Massive government intervention in the economy had turned chronic unemployment into a labour shortage. As unemployment disappeared workers became more confident about asserting their rights on the job. Canadian voters also began to show their support for the left-wing political ideas that had been floating around in the last few decades. People who had seen government intervention end a depression to fight a war were not prepared to return to the days of laissez-faire when the war ended.

It was to end the strike waves and to stop the growing support for the leftist parties that the Liberals committed themselves to Keynesianism in the final years of the war. Programs and policies introduced during this age include: family allowance, the legal right to strike, the requirement that employers bargain with certified unions, a government policy of full employment, unemployment insurance, Canadian Pension Plan, medicare, and the Canada Assistance Plan (a national standard of welfare). This period is sometimes referred to as the era of the postwar labour accord, when large business agreed to deal with unions, while unions were able to improve living standards out of an increasingly productive economy.

The 1970s also brought a new phenomenon not encompassed in Keynesian thought—stagflation: high inflation and rising unemployment at the same time. Increased global competition and declining profits during the 1970s signalled the beginning of the end of the accord.

(Continued)

Ideas in Action: A Short Economic History Of the Twentieth Century

The Landslide: 1975 to the Present

The 1970s were a period of extended conflict and turmoil. Governments began abandoning many elements of the postwar accord. For example: freezing wages and legislating ends to strikes. Corporations wishing to change the political landscape seized upon the ideas of Milton Friedman. Think tanks bankrolled by corporations began to make the argument for neo-classical ideas. Some of the targets of the neo-conservatives were: the large public sector, unions, special interest groups, and expensive social programs.

By the 1980s the neo-classical economists had won the war of ideas. They held office in London, Ottawa, and Washington. Their policies involved: high interest rates that kept unemployment high, restrictions on trade union rights, regressive taxation, and drastic reduction in the size of the public sector. The use of these policies has caused an increase in poverty, a twenty-year decline in living standards, chronic unemployment, and what is now termed jobless growth.

The authors of these policies often acknowledge that this is strong medicine, but they say that short-term pain is needed to set the stage for long-term growth. In short that there are no alternatives. Challenges have been and continue to be made to the "common sense" of this era. The AFB provides a process in which people with quite different ideas can prove that there are alternatives.

Exercise 2:
Looking at a Family Budget

This exercise centres around a mythical Canadian family, with two parents, both working to pay of their $75,000 home, three children at home, a grandmother in a nursing home and the need to supplement the income of a brother (uncle) with disabilities. Near the end of 1998 there is a family crisis. The eight year old son, Martin, has been diagnosed with a learning disorder. The public school system does not have the resources to deal with the problem. The family has a chance to enrol him in a special tutoring program that has had considerable success in helping students like him stay in school. The one year program costs $10,000. There are a number of ways the family can respond. Each reflects the family's underlying values. Your assignment is to analyze the three budgets and answer the following questions:

• What are the choices each family has made?

• What will the impact of these choices be?

• What values does each budget represent?

Family's 1998 Budget

(All figures in thousands of dollars.)

REVENUE

Father's salary	50
Mother's salary	25
TOTAL INCOME	**75**

EXPENDITURES

Basic Family Costs:	
Food	12
Taxes	20
Clothing	3
Transportation	3
Utilities, Maintenance	5
Other (Insurance, Charity Entertainment, Pet)	6
Individual Costs:	
Michael's (3) day care	3
Martin's (8) allowance	1
Mary's (17) allowance	2
Mother's nursing home	5
Disabled brother (Supplement welfare)	3
TOTAL EXPENDITURE	**63**

Operating Balance	12
Debt Payments:	
Mortgage Interest	6
Mortgage Principal	6
Surplus / (Deficit)	0
Assets / (Debt)	
Mortgage owed	(25)
Home	75

Three Budgets for a Family Emergency

Father's salary	50	50	50
Mother's salary	25	25	25
Rent Room			4
Sale of House	50		
Total Income	125	75	79

EXPENDITURES

BASIC FAMILY COSTS

Rent	7		
Food	9	12	11
Taxes	20	20	20
Clothing	3	3	3
Transportation	3	3	3
Utilities, Maintenance	5	5	7
Other (Insurance, Charity Entertainment, Pet)	6	6	5

INDIVIDUAL COSTS

Michael's (3) day care	3	3	3
Martin's program	10		10
Martin's (8) allowance	1	1	1
Mary's (17) allowance	2	2	2
Mother's nursing home	5	5	5
Disabled brother (Supplement welfare)	3	3	3
Total Expenditure	77	63	73

OPERATING BALANCE	48	12	6

DEBT PAYMENTS

Bank loan			6
Mortgage Interest		6	6
Mortgage Principal		6	6

SURPLUS / (DEFICIT)	48	0	(12)

ASSETS / (DEBT)

Mortgage owed	0	(19)	(19)
Home	0	77	77
Savings	48		
Bank loan			(7)

Values in a Government Budget

This is a real, if simplified, version of the federal budget.

The Martin Budget 1998-99

(All numbers are in billions of dollars.)

REVENUE

Personal Income Tax	71.0
Corporate Income Tax	20.5
EI Premiums	18.6
GST	20.9
Customs and Excise Taxes	11.1
Other Revenue	8.9
TOTAL REVENUE	151.0

EXPENDITURES

Old Age Security	22.9
EI Payments	12.6
Transfers to Governments	19.5
Direct Program Spending	17.0
Transfers to Crown Corps	3.8
Defence	7.9
Other	20.8
TOTAL PROGRAM SPENDING	104.5
Operating Balance	46.5
Public Debt Charges	43.5
Total Expenditures	148.0
Surplus / (Deficit)	3.0
Net Public Debt	583.2

Values in a Government Budget: Definitions

PERSONAL INCOME TAX

The amount of money the government expects to receive from taxing individuals. In Canada the income tax system is supposed to be progressive. The more you make, the higher your taxation.

CORPORATE INCOME TAX

The amount of money the government expects to receive from taxing corporations. The amount that corporations contribute to the national revenue has been declining.

EI PREMIUMS

These are the premiums that workers and employers pay into the Employment Insurance Fund. If you look on the expenditure side you will see that the government was planning to collect far more than is spent on EI.

THE GOODS AND SERVICES TAX (GST)

Critics of this tax point out that it falls on everyone when they make purchases, regardless of their ability to pay.

EXPENDITURES

Old age security are payments made to senior citizens. EI payments are the payments made to people who are receiving Employment Insurance. Transfers to government cover some of the government's most significant spending (health, post-secondary education, welfare, and equalization payments).

DIRECT PROGRAM SPENDING

This is spending through government programs, such as agricultural subsidies, aboriginal health, industrial and regional development programs, international aid, etc.

TRANSFERS TO CROWN CORPS

This includes funding to Crown corporations such as the Canadian Broadcasting Corporation, Atomic Energy Canada, etc.

DEFENCE

This is funding for the Canadian Armed Forces.

Exercise 3: The Martin Budget and Two Alternatives

Here is the 1998-99 federal budget as released by Paul Martin. Go over it line by line and get a sense of what he is doing. Then look at the other two versions printed in columns A and B.

Unlike the Family Budget exercise we looked at earlier, this exercise presents two alternatives for the same year. Compare the three budgets and note the differences. Use the second page of the handout to help you identify what choices are being made. Think also about which economic thinkers you might identify with those choices. Think about the impact of the three budgets on Canadians and on Canadian business.

What are the choices that are being made in each budget?

What will the impacts of these choices be?

What values does each budget represent?

The Martin Budget
and Two Alternatives

(All figures are in billions of dollars.)

	MARTIN	A	B
REVENUE			
Personal Income Tax	71.0	69.0	71.0
Corporate Income Tax	20.5	18.0	31.0
EI Premiums	18.6	17.0	18.0
GST	20.9	23.0	20.0
Excise Taxes	11.1	11.0	11.0
Other Revenue	8.9	9.0	9.0
Total Revenue	151.0	147.0	160.0
EXPENDITURES			
Old Age Security	22.9	21.0	24.0
EI Payments	12.6	13.0	15.0
Transfers to Governments	19.5	18.0	31.0
Direct Program Spending	17.0	18.0	17.0
Crown Corps	3.8	4.0	4.0
Defence	7.9	9.0	10.0
Other	20.8	17.0	19.0
Total Program Spending	104.5	100.0	120.0
Operating Balance	46.5	47.0	40.0
Public Debt Charges	43.5	43.0	41.0
Total Expenditures	148.0	143.0	161.0
Surplus / (Deficit)	3.0	4.0	(1)
Net Public Debt	583.2	580.0	587.0

How Job Creation can Affect Other AFB Goals

The object of this exercise is to explore the way that efforts designed to implement one of the goals of the AFB can affect, positively or negatively, other goals. The column on the left lists some macroeconomic job creation measures. Along the top of the chart are possible effects of those measures. They are also the goals the AFB is committed to. Discuss this with the other members of your group.

This exercise helps us to see the importantance of balancing one's prioritites in the process of making a budget.

	Create Jobs	Poverty Alleviation	Reduce Debt and Deficit	Make Taxation Fairer	Protect Social Services
Government Buys More Goods and Services					
Government Hires More Employees					
Government Redistributes Wealth from Wealthy to Poor					

Exercise 5: The Impacts of
Different Forms of Financing

Take a look at the chart below. Down the left hand column are a number of macroeconomic measures that can be used to finance job creation. Write down the ways that you think that each job creation measure might affect, positively and negatively, the other AFB goals. Try to see where these measures would fit together and where they might be working at cross purposes.

	Create Jobs	Poverty Alleviation	Reduce Debt and Deficit	Make Taxation Fairer	Protect Social Services
Government Lowers Interest Rates					
Government Raises Taxes					
Government Runs a Deficit					
Government Funds Increase out of Growth					
Government Finances Debt by Selling Bonds					
Bank of Canada Finances a Portion of the Deficit					

Canada's War on Inflation

Inflation is a General Increase in Prices

High Interest Rates Slow Inflation

Borrowing to manufacture decreases
Demand falls
Prices fall
Consumer borrowing falls

High Interest Rates Create Deficits and Debt

Demand decreases
Unemployment rises
Tax revenues fall
Deficits grow
Debt servicing charges rise
Debt skyrockets

The War On Inflation
Caused Canada's Debt

AFB's Five Year Plan 1997-2002

(All figures in billions of dollars.)

Fiscal Years	1997 (Forecast)	1998	1999	2000	2001	2002
Revenue	148.2	160.2	167.3	179.0	191.6	205.0
Program Spending	105.8	118.7	127.1	139.7	153.1	167.4
Debt Service Charges	43.8	41.5	39.2	38.4	37.5	36.6
Total Spending	149.6	160.2	166.3	178.0	190.6	204.0
Surplus (Deficit)	**(1.4)**	**0.0**	**1.0**	**1.0**	**1.0**	**1.0**
Net Debt	585	585	584	583	582	581
GDP	849	900	958	1025	1097	1174
Debt as % of GDP	68.9	65.0	60.9	56.8	53.0	49.5

AFB Program Spending

(All figures in millions of dollars.)

	1997-98	1998-99	1999-2000
NATIONAL SOCIAL INVESTMENT FUNDS			
Health Care Fund	6664	9407	10500
Post Secondary Education Fund	2273	3137	3600
Income Support Fund	5562	7500	8200
Child Care Investment Fund	350	896	1500
Housing Investment Fund	1863	2263	2500
Retirement Fund	22300	23497	24700
Unemployment Insurance Fund	13200	14200	15200
DEPARTMENTAL SPENDING AND OTHER			
Equity Participation Fund	0	100	150
Disabilities-VRDP	168	198	204
First Nations	4308	4808	5308
Common Security (Foreign Affairs and Defence)	13138	12808	12628
Agriculture	1505	1555	1600
Industry (including Infrastructure)	3837	4337	4600
Environment	517	1550	1570
Natural Resources	696	846	981
Fisheries	1077	1127	1161
Transport	1753	1753	1805
Immigration	652	887	913
Human Resources and Training	3544	4195	4321
Justice	3270	3275	3368
Culture	2524	2825	3004
Veterans' Pensions	1921	1840	1840
Equalization	8300	8400	8600
Transfers to Territories	1100	1196	1232
Government Services and Other	5278	6100	7615
TOTAL PROGRAM SPENDING	**105 800**	**118 700**	**127 100**

AFB Tax Revenue

(All figures in millions of dollars.)

TAX EXPENDITURE REFORM

Full Inclusion of Capital Gaims in Income	1180
Eliminate Dividend Tax Credit	640
Integrate Corporate and Personal Tax for Small Business	346

CAPITAL GAINS EXEMPTIONS

Restrict $500,000 Farm Assets Exemption	153
Restrict $500,000 Small Business Exemption	548
Eliminate Capital Gains Freeze, Family Trusts	300

DISALLOWANCE OF CERTAIN DEDUCTIONS

Meals and Entertainment (Corporate and Personal)	305
Lobbying Expenses	50
Salary in Excess of Ten Times Average Wage	50
Restrict Eligibility for Scientific Research Credit	508

INCOME AND WEALTH TAX REFORM

Wealth Transer Tax, Estates over $1,000,000	2925
Increase Top Income Tax Rate from 29 to 30 percent	510
Add New Tax Brackets at $100,000 and $150,000	775

GREEN TAXES

$4 / Tonne Carbon Fuel Tax	500
Eliminate Tax Preferences for Oil and Gas Development	500

OTHER

Restore Non-Resident Withholding Tax to Treaty Rates	411
Introduce Minimum Tax on Profitable Corporations	400
Extend GST to Brokerage and Other Financial Services	190
Restore Tobacco Taxation to pre-1995 Level	495

ONE TIME TAXES

Surtax on Private Financial Institutions	1500
Enhanced Enforcement of Tax Regulations	600

Exercise 7: Paul Martin vs. the AFB

We have put the 1998-99 AFB and the 1997-98 Martin budget side by side. (When we put together the AFB each year, we always begin with the previous year's federal government budget.)

We have also added a number of other economic statistics: the gross domestic product (GDP), the unemployment rate, the real interest rate (adjusted for inflation), and the inflation rate. We've also added one extremely useful tool. We have taken the main areas of the budget and expressed them as a percentage of the GDP. The GDP is the total value of the goods and services produced in any given year in a country. It is a measuring stick that allows for clear comparisons between financial years. It also allows comparisons between countries. The European Union has set a standard that a country's debt is acceptable if it is 60 percent of GDP. Looking at the chart showing the two federal budgets, where can you see evidence of:

- Job creation strategies?
- The attitudes toward debt / deficit held by the budget makers?
- Support for social programs?

What can you say by looking at:

- Differences in the expenditure side?
- Differences in the economic indicators at the bottom of the page (e.g. inflation rate, unemployment, interest rates, etc.)?

Compare revenue as a percentage of GDP. What does this tell you?

Comparison of Martin Budget and AFB

	MARTIN 1997-98	AFB 1998-99
Program Spending		
National Social Investment Funds		
Health Care Fund	6.7	9.4
Post-Secondary Education Fund	2.3	3.1
Income Support Fund	5.5	7.5
Child Care Investment Fund	0.3	0.9
Housing Investment Fund	1.9	2.3
Retirement Fund	22.3	23.5
Unemployment Insurance Fund	13.2	14.2
Sub-Total NSIFs	52.2	60.9
Departmental Spending / Other:	53.6	57.8
Total Program Spending	105.8	118.7
Total Revenue	148.2	160.2
Operating Balance	42.4	41.5
Public Debt Charges	43.8	41.5
Total Expenditures	149.6	160.2
Surplus / (Deficit)	(1.4)	0.0
Net Public Debt	585.0	585.0
AS A PERCENTAGE OF GDP		
Revenues	17.5	17.8
Program Spending	12.5	13.2
Debt Charges	5.2	4.6
Deficit	0.1	0.0
Net Public Debt	68.9	65.0
ECONOMIC INDICATORS		
GDP	849.0	900.0
Real Interest Rate	2.4%	1.5%
Unemployment Rate	8.9%	7.9%
Inflation Rate	1.5%	2.0%

Reflection and Evaluation

We want to give you 10 - 15 minutes at the end of the workshop to reflect on what you've learned and help us evaluate our methods. Can you take a few minutes to think about each of the following questions? Write down as little or as much as you want, and leave the questionnaire with us when you leave.

1. We had four objectives. What did you learn in each of the following areas?

    a. Basic economic literacy

    b. Critique of the values that are now creating budgets

    c. Understanding the Alternative Federal Budget

    d. A change to express alternatives of your own

2. What did you learn of significance to you that's not included in the above list?

3. Which was your favourite activity in the workshop?

4. Which was your least favourite?

5. What things did we miss? Something that was not covered that you would have like to have seen covered?

6. What do you take away with you from this workshop?